AMERICAN JURISPRUDENCE

Al & Erestine,
with Fond Memories
your Friend
Tom Todd

AMERICAN JURISPRUDENCE

AN ANALYSIS OF ITS HISTORICAL ROOTS

THOMAS DAVIDSON TODD

WHALER BOOKS

Buena Vista, VA

1 3   5   7   9   10   8   6   4   2

Library of Congress Control Number: 2021923332

American Jurisprudence
By Thomas Davidson Todd
p. cm.

1. Political Science—History & Theory
2. Political Science—American Government: Judicial Branch
3. Political Science—Colonialism & Post-Colonialism

I. Todd, Thomas 1934– II. Title.
ISBN 13: 978-1-7378864-1-9 (softcover : alk. paper)

Design by Karen Bowen

Whaler Books
An imprint of
Mariner Media, Inc.
131 West 21st Street
Buena Vista, VA 24416
Tel: 540-264-0021
www.marinermedia.com

Printed in the United States of America
This book is printed on acid-free paper meeting the
requirements of the American Standard for
Permanence of Paper for Printed Library Materials.

The purpose of this book is to identify those forces which form the historical taproot of the advocacy system of jurisprudence; and subsequently, to determine if history sustains the author's contention that the environmental influence of the primeval wilderness was a pregnating and intimidating force, that not only projected a dominating aura over a multitude of less potent forces—to which all of the colonists were subjected—but, that by its destructive relationship with the cultural shackles of the human mind released the full force of individualism to impact upon the embryonic heritage of English jurisprudence—consequently—molding it into a uniquely American system.

–Thomas Davidson Todd

TABLE OF CONTENTS

Chapter Four: Virginia and the Birth of American Jurisprudence, 1776–1803 63

LIST OF FIGURES

CHAPTER ONE

American and English Jurisprudence in the Twentieth Century: Their Common Roots

The scene is an English meadow in a long ago forgotten year—perhaps 1070 A.D.—after William the Conqueror and his Normans had successfully invaded England. Several men are stationed in a circle surrounding two others dressed as if for combat. It appears to be just an ordinary duel—but no, it is actually a trial: a "Trial by Battle," in which the two opposing sides, the defendant and the plaintiff, are represented by their respective champions.[1] Now we see another trial scene, this time it is an American courtroom in the year 1980. The judge sits behind a high bench at the front of the room, while a dozen steps or so in front of him there are two separate tables; the defendant and his champion are seated at one table and the plaintiff and his champion at the other. These champions are called attorneys, or lawyers, and their fight against each other is being conducted by verbal and written words while the judge—the trier of the law—arbitrates the dispute. Off to one side a group of citizens, known as the jury, listens to the presentations. They are the triers of fact—deciding the issue of who is right and wrong. And in criminal trials, the guilt or innocence of the accused.[2] Both scenes represent the "Advocacy/ Accusatorial" system of jurisprudence utilized throughout the English-speaking world[3]: the beginning[4] and the present.[5] Thus, only the nature of the combat has changed—the philosophy remains unaltered. Although in theory the justice that emerges from the judicial system is supposed to be identifiable with the truth, in practice the two may or may not be familiar with each other. The competitive individualism that characterizes the western world, and the United States in particular, tends to be dominant over the desire for the truth as attorneys fight for their conflicting interests. We are of course viewing only the theory side of our judicial system, because in the area of criminal cases, only about ten percent ever reach the trial stage. This is in reference to the United States only. The remainder are settled by "plea bargaining" between the prosecutor and the defense lawyer.[6]

Anywhere within the aforementioned area of the world the purpose of the judicial system remains the same:

> ...to resolve disputes. The manner of judicial disputes resolution is quite unique. That system is one of arbitration of individual cases through an adversary process. The courts act as arbitrators, while the parties to the dispute advocate their opposing interests. In criminal cases, one interest is the protection of society through prosecution of those believed to have committed crimes. The opposing interest is the protection of the rights of the accused through the demonstration of a reasonable doubt of guilt.[7]

The primary foundation of the advocacy system, inherited from Anglo-Saxon England, is the presumption of innocence until proven guilty beyond a reasonable doubt. This is the taproot

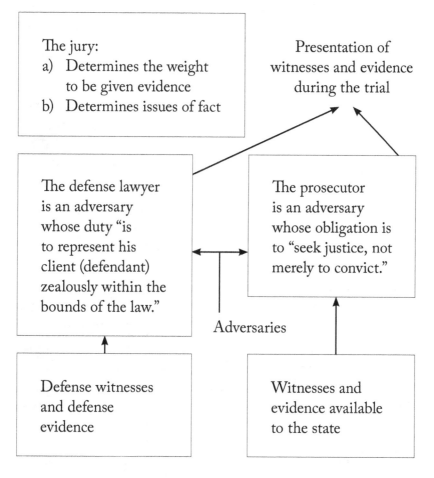

The trial judge:
a) Determines questions of law
b) Determines questions of fact if the trial is conducted without a jury
c) "has the responsibility for safeguarding both the rights of the accused and the interests of the public in the administration of criminal justice."

The jury:
a) Determines the weight to be given evidence
b) Determines issues of fact

Presentation of witnesses and evidence during the trial

The defense lawyer is an adversary whose duty "is to represent his client (defendant) zealously within the bounds of the law."

The prosecutor is an adversary whose obligation is to "seek justice, not merely to convict."

Adversaries

Defense witnesses and defense evidence

Witnesses and evidence available to the state

FIGURE 1:   Source: *Criminal Evidence, Principles, Cases and Readings,* Thomas J. Gardner, West Publishing Co., St. Paul, MN, December 1977.

of the advocacy tree of justice; and consequently, is the basis for the continuous and careful scrutiny that has been the ever-attentive watch dog of individual rights in the United States. Numbered among these rights are the writ of habeas corpus, the right to cross-examine witnesses and to confront your accuser, and protection against unlawful seizures and self-incrimination. The judge in the Advocacy/Accusatorial system is entitled to participate in questioning the witnesses, but normally restricts himself to arbitrating the dispute as the trier of the law.[8]

The grand jury, which has been charged with the primary purpose of deciding whether sufficient evidence exist to warrant bringing an alleged offender to trial, has become for all practical purposes the body appendix of the American judicial system. Normally its function on the state level has been fulfilled by the method of "information"—the filing of an affidavit of charges.[9] Its common usage is more on the federal level where the 5th Amendment guaranteed the right of a grand jury.[10] In Wales and England its usage was eliminated by the Administration of Justice Act of 1933. The usage of the trial or petit jury was also reduced by the aforementioned legislative act. Consequently, in only five percent of the civil cases does this judicial body engage in its traditional role in Wales and England.[11]

A jury is always impaneled in English criminal cases where a plea of "not guilty" is entered to an indictable offense. Such a jury consists of ten to twelve citizens, who since 1971, no longer have to arrive at a unanimous verdict. Depending on the numbers of jurors, the vote can be ten to two, eleven to one, or nine to one. The basis for the reduction in usage of the petit jury was found in the belief that English judges are more efficient than juries, the desire for speedy trials and—probably the primary factor—that litigants in British courts pay the juror's fee out of their own pockets.[12]

In the United States we find eighty percent of all the world's jury trials. The 6th Amendment to the federal constitution makes the use of a jury mandatory in all felony cases unless waived by the defendant, and in all civil cases over twenty dollars. The Seventh amendment grants the same requirement unless waived. The states, however, vary from no jury to a mixture of judge and jury in civil cases. Except for some state juries, a unanimous verdict is required for a valid verdict to be recognized.[13]

There is a vast difference in the court structures of these two English speaking nations, the United States and England. The latter has only one judicial system, while the United States, because of its federal system of government, has a dual system; or perhaps for greater accuracy, it should be described as fifty-one different systems. The judicial system of each state and that of the national government are distinct entities; although, through the appellate process they merge in submission to the decisions of the United States Supreme Court.[14]

The court systems of thirty-three states have the justice of the peace as the lowest court of the judicial hierarchy.[15] This individual, who frequently is not a lawyer, is normally elected for a term of two to six years in a county or township. His duties are a combination of legal, administrative, and legislative functions, with the judicial duties concerning only minor criminal and civil cases. Because of his dependency on the fee for conviction, the justice is casually referred to as the "Justice for the Plaintiff."[16] He acts only in an examining role if an offense is a felony.[17]

The next court frequently found in a state court system is the municipal court. Normally its original (trial) jurisdiction is limited to civil cases under $500 to $1,000, and to misdemeanors where criminal jurisdiction is authorized. It is sometimes called the traffic court, city court, night court, or police court. At the next level there is the county court. It is a court of original jurisdiction responsible for hearing all civil cases above those authorized for the inferior courts, all felony cases, certain misdemeanors, and in some cases, inheritance and probate disputes. This is the first court level where juries will be utilized. Although the county court is predominately a trial court, it may on occasion hear appeals from inferior courts.[18]

At the next higher level is located the first court of appeals. This court receives and hears appeals from decisions of the inferior courts. Although its decision terminates most cases it is possible to carry a case on to the state's court of last resort. Usually this court is called the supreme court. It is concerned with major questions emitting from the inferior trial courts; by way of the intermediate appeals court by writ of appeal or certiorari. Its functions are strictly appellate. In certain cases the state supreme court will accept a case directly from an inferior trial court if the matter is of sufficient importance. The appellate courts are not usually concerned with the guilt or innocence, the right or wrong of a particular case; but rather with the correct application and constitutionality of a law as interpreted and applied by the trial judge or law enforcement personnel.[19]

The federal court system consists of two basic types: the constitutional courts as established by Article III of

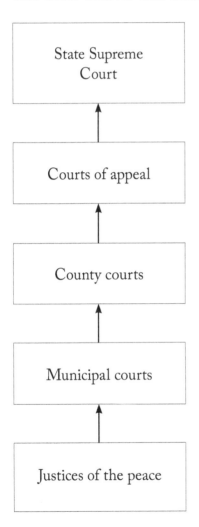

FIGURE 2: TYPICAL STATE COURT SYSTEM, 1980

the United States Constitution, of which the Supreme Court of the United States is the only one; and the remainder, which are legislative courts, because they were established by Congress under the authority of Article I—the legislative article of the constitution.[20] These are further identified as trial and appellate courts.

The trial courts are the magistrates, the lowest federal court in the national judicial hierarchy, and at the next level above, the district courts. The office of the magistrate replaced the former judicial office of U.S. Commissioners in 1971. This court has original and limited jurisdiction; the occupant must be a licensed attorney, and is appointed for a term of eight years by the district court judges. The jurisdiction of the U.S. magistrates is mainly criminal, and involves the conduct of preliminary proceedings and the conduct of trials involving petty and minor offenses; that is, if the defendant consents to be tried. A demand for a jury trial forces a case into the district court.[21]

The U.S. district courts have cognizance over federal law violations within their districts and on the high seas, over all admiralty and maritime cases,

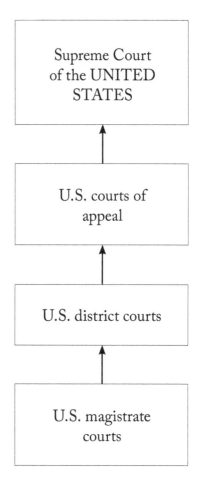

FIGURE 3: FEDERAL COURT SYSTEM OF THE UNITED STATES, 1980

cognizance of seizures made on land and water, and jurisdiction of all suits involving consuls and vice-consuls. Their jurisdiction takes cognizance of both civil and criminal matters. Normally presided over by one judge, cases involving the constitutionality of state laws require two district judges and one court of appeals judge. There are ninety-four of these courts.[22]

FIGURE 4: THE UNITED STATES COURTS OF APPEALS
AND THE UNITED STATES DISTRICT COURTS

The numerals indicate the various courts of appeals and the heavy lines represent the jurisdictional boundaries of each circuit. The broken lines represent jurisdictional boundaries of district courts in states having more than one district.

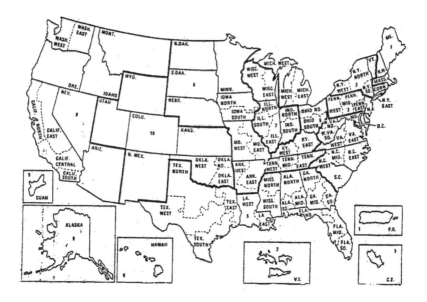

Source: The United States Courts, Their Jurisdiction and Work, Committee on the Judiciary, House of Representatives.

The first level appellate courts are the U.S. courts of appeals. There are eleven of these courts with three to fifteen judges in each area of jurisdiction. Such an area is called a circuit, and includes three or more states. Both criminal and civil appeals are taken cognizance of by the courts of appeals.[23]

At the top of federal court system is the Supreme Court of the United States, consisting by tradition of nine justices. Although primarily an appellate court, it does enjoy original jurisdiction in certain specified areas. Being the sole judge of which individual cases it will entertain, the Supreme Court can exercise original jurisdiction in any case involving disputes between states, suits brought by the representatives of foreign governments, disputes between a state and the national government, and suits between states and citizens of another state or country. In some, but not all of the above suits, the courts has exclusive jurisdiction. Appeals to the Supreme Court can originate in the highest court of each state, the U.S. district courts, the U.S. courts of appeals, and from several of the special federal courts.[24] It has the final decision on the constitutionality of any law, state or federal, which it takes cognizance of as result of a specific case awaiting its judgement. It is the only court of last resort in the world which has that authority.[25]

The British court system is much simpler in that it is designed to fit their unitary form of government. The English Parliament, in the 19th century, established a system of courts that are still intact today. Entitled "The County Courts Act of 1846" it created the latter type courts to deal with civil cases where small sums of money were at issue. The amount was raised to 750 lbs. (approximately $1,500) in 1959. The lowest criminal court is that of the magistrate, equivalent to the American justice of the peace. Misdemeanors are tried in this court, the indictable offences—which we call felonies—are heard in the Crown Court. Civil disputes are processed through a different court system. If the value is less than 750 lbs., jurisdiction is assumed

FIGURE 5: COURT SYSTEM OF GREAT BRITAIN, 1980

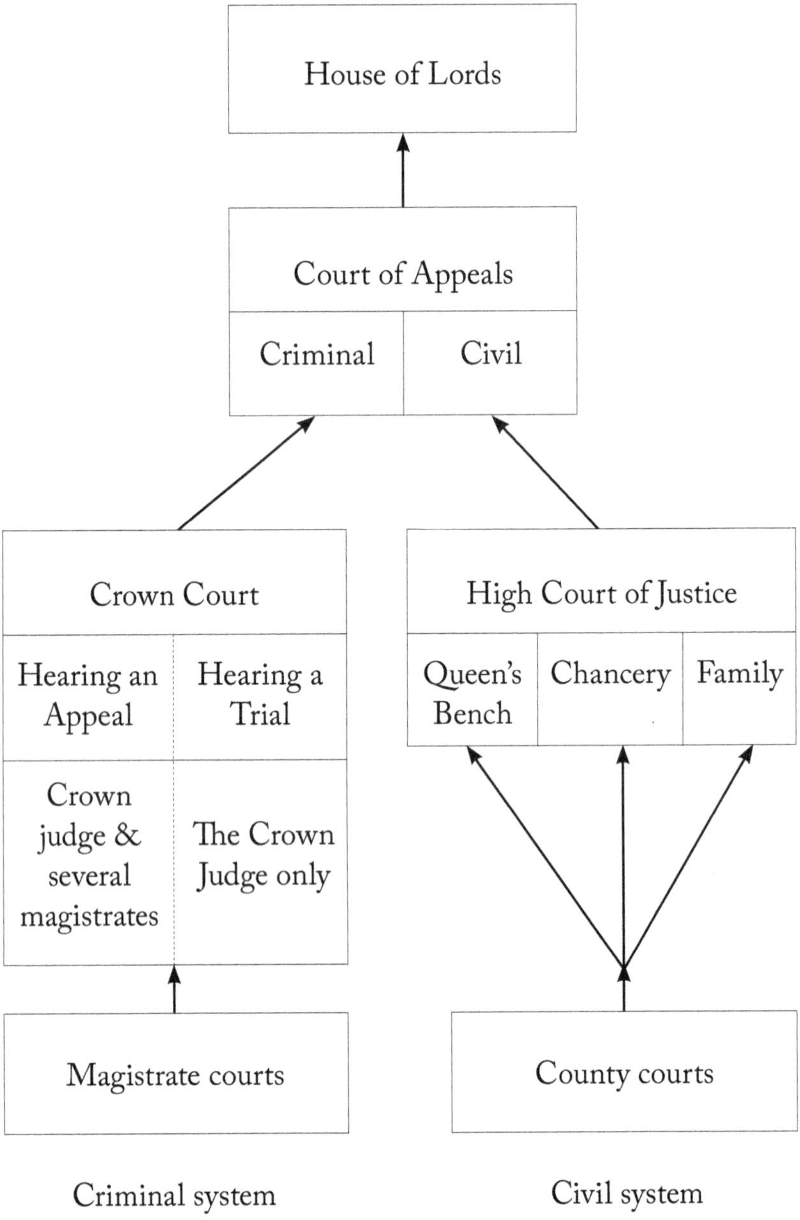

House of Lords

Court of Appeals	
Criminal	Civil

Crown Court		High Court of Justice		
Hearing an Appeal	Hearing a Trial	Queen's Bench	Chancery	Family
Crown judge & several magistrates	The Crown Judge only			

Magistrate courts	County courts

Criminal system   Civil system

Applicable to England and Wales only; Northern Ireland and Scotland have their own court systems.

by a county court; above said amount, the High Court of Justice has cognizance of the case in question. This court is divided into three different divisions, and all cases, whether coming to the court's attention as a case under appeal or as a case of original jurisdiction (over 750 lbs. value), are assigned to the appropriate section of the court for hearing. The sections are: the Queen's Bench Court, the Chancery Court, and the Family Court.[26]

The next court in the British court system is the Court of Appeals—the level where the criminal and civil judicial routes first converge. The joining here, however, is not yet complete, since the court is divided into criminal and civil sections. Only in the court of last resort, the House of Lords, do the criminal and civil court system finally merge completely. It is to be noted, that unlike the United States, the final appellate court in England is primarily a legislative body—a house of the Parliament of the United Kingdom.[27]

In the United States judges are either appointed or elected to the bench; in England, appointment is the sole method utilized to elevate an attorney to the bench, or to raise a judge to a higher court. At the federal level in the United States, all judges secure their positions by appointment from the President of the United States subject to the approval of the Senate. Prior to the appointment, however, three traditional factors exercise considerable influence on the chief magistrate's choice. First of all, there is consultation with the senators and other officials, the congressmen in question, the governors involved, etc.; secondly, since 1946 the committee of the American Bar Association on Federal Judiciary investigates all possible candidates, and then submits a written report with its rating of either Eminently well qualified, Well qualified, Qualified, or Not qualified; and, thirdly, in the case of the Supreme Court, requesting recommendations of the sitting justices.[28]

In Britain—England and Wales only—all judges are selected by the Lord Chancellor, the senior law figure of the government and the judicial hierarchy, with almost no political considerations influencing the selection. The Lord chancellor is also the Speaker of the House of Lords (the court of last resort) and a member of the British cabinet. In his position as the judiciary leader, he combines the three powers of the executive, the legislature, and the judiciary. His office is older than that of the Prime Minister, to whom he is subordinate.

Since 1907 political considerations have scarcely caused a ripple as all political parties have acquiesced in its absence from judicial selections for the courts. A member of an opposition party, who is eminently qualified for a judicial vacancy is just as likely to be appointed as a loyal member of the party in power. Except for inquiries of sitting judges, whose judicial opinion of a particular candidate is often solicited, recommendations of political figures is neither sought nor offered.[29]

The election of judges is uniquely American in this modern world of the twenty-first century. At the state and lower governmental levels eighty-two percent of the judges are elected by either the state legislatures, or by the people themselves.[30]

There is also a wide contrast between the mother country and her American sibling as to the qualifications required to be a judge. In the United States the only requirement for obtaining a judgeship is a law degree from an accredited law school; and in many cases, even this requirement, is one of tradition rather than of statutory or constitutional law. Consequently, many American judges approach their courtroom for the first time with little or no judicial experience. Among the one hundred individuals who served on the United States Supreme Court between 1789 and 1974, only twenty-two had at least ten years of previous experience as a judge, and forty-two had no judicial experience at all.[31]

England, to the contrary, goes even further than might be expected, in that they first of all divide their attorneys into two professional groups: the solicitors and the barristers. An

English attorney cannot be both. The solicitors are the most numerous, and it is they who conduct about 95% of the legal business of the country, and, who deal directly with the public. The transformation of the advocacy philosophy into the trial by battle of the modern court trial is the role of the barrister. In addition to being a court room trial lawyer, he also acts as a consultant for solicitors who seek his advice on difficult legal questions. Although the solicitor can try cases in the county courts, he hires a barrister for any case being called before a higher court.[32]

In the United States diversity has been a major problem confronting our judiciary for years.[33] The American judicial systems reflect the same decentralization influences and tendency for local control that is a major characteristic of all our governmental and law enforcement bodies. In marked contrast, however, to this concept of decentralization, is the American acceptance of the public prosecutor. The English, today as throughout their history, leave criminal charges to the local police who hire private attorneys to prosecute their cases. And, should the police fail to press criminal charges in a case, a private citizen may sponsor the criminal charge(s) against an alleged offender.[34]

It is only by peering back into the mist of our common past that we come to understand the blend of statutory and common law. The first is legislative law; the type that has been promulgated into written codes. The common law, to the contrary, is not written; but rather, is based on the judicial precedence and traditions of antiquity. The common law is basic to both nations. Its philosophical foundation is the theory that similar cases should be interpreted in the same manner. This philosophy is epitomized in the doctrine of "stare decisis—to follow the precedent."[35]

To find the roots of the "common law," the taproot of the entire Advocacy/Accusatorial system of justice, we must go back to that point in time immediately following the year 893 A.D., when King Alfred finally expelled the Danes from his kingdom. Society had been destroyed to such an extent that no one was safe, in or out of their homes. As a remedy to this wretched state the king divided the kingdom into counties, the counties into hundreds, and the hundreds into tithings. Each tithing consisted of ten households, and the head of each household was responsible for the conduct of all persons who were members— even guests if they stayed more than three days. Every household in a tithing was responsible for the behavior of the other households. One man, out of each tithing, was appointed as a tithingman. He was summoned by the hundred to answer for his tithing if a member thereof committed an offense.[36] When a dispute or problem arose within a tithing, the tithingman summoned the other members to resolve the situation. A party affected adversely could appeal to the hundred. Likewise, cases effecting more than one tithing were heard by the hundred. The hundred consisted of ten tithings and met at stated intervals. According to David Hume, the noted 17th century political theorist, the birth of the jury can be found in this ancient system of social control.[37]

Each county, which consisted of ten hundreds, had a court which met twice a year. This court, which was presided over by the local bishop and an alderman, consisted of all the freeholders (landowners) of the county.[38] The court heard cases involving parties from two or more hundreds, and appeals from the courts of the hundreds. The court of last resort was the King's Council.[39]

It is within that code of laws enacted by King Athelstan (924–939 A.D.) that we discover the first indication of "Trial by Ordeal." The fourth law of the code states:

> Concerning treachery to a Lord. And we pronounced concerning treachery to a Lord, that he (who is accused) is to forfeit his life if he cannot deny it or is afterwards convicted at the three-fold ordeal.[40]

The first mention of the specific details of an ordeal is found in the twenty-third law of this code which states the following:

> If anyone pledges the ordeal, he is then to come three days before a priest whose duty it is to consecrate it, and live off bread and water and salt and vegetables until he shall go to it, and be present at Mass on each of those three days, and make his offering and go to communion on the day on which he shall go to the ordeal, and swear then the oath that he is guiltless of that charge according to the common law, before he goes to the ordeal.
>
> And if it is (the ordeal of) water, he is to sink one and a half ells on the rope; if it is the ordeal of iron, it is to be three days before the hand is unbound.[41]

William the Conqueror and his Normans introduced a new form of trial to England: "Trial by Battle." This method, however, was reserved for disputes between Normans; not between a Norman and an Anglo-Saxon, nor between Anglo-Saxon adversaries.[42]

Leaping forward to the time of Henry the II we find the first clear indications of the beginnings of judicial proceedings as we know them today. The documents which issued from his throne, not only created new legal landmarks, but gathered together the laws and customs of the past.[43] In 1166 A.D. King Henry II held a council at Clarendon, England; and from this council he issued the first great legislative enactment of his remarkable reign: "The Assize of Clarendon."[44] This legislative session confirmed the existence of the grand jury, referred therein as juries of presentment and recognition. This "accusing jury" was to have criminal jurisdiction within the hundred. The ancient procedures of compurgation (the practice of clearing an accused person of a charge by having a number of people swear to a belief in his innocence), trial by ordeal and battle, were now to be supplemented by evidence pertaining to the record and reputation of the accused.[45]

Then in 1176 A.D. the king summoned another council to gather at Northhampton, England. Entitled "The Assize of Northhampton," this body increased the powers of the judges at the expense of the county sheriffs. Also enacted were six new judicial circuits with two or more judges for each circuit. These new circuits appeared to be larger judicial areas than the counties—each circuit probably encompassing two or more.[46]

The next document in Henry II's reign is a legal treatise commonly referred as "Granville," actually entitled "Concerning the Laws and Customs of the Kingdom of England," and written about 1190 A.D. We'll observe that in this time frame there was increasingly a choice between the newer and milder methods of judicial procedures, and the older violent ways that were gradually being replaced.[47] In a dispute over ownership of land, for instance, the party residing thereon had his choice of the method: trial by battle, or submit the issue to the King's Grand Assize. If the possessor of the land elected the latter method of the King's Grand Assize, the plaintiff had to abide by the choice or lose his suit. If however, the plaintiff declined on the ground that he and the defendant were of the same blood, and such was determined to be true, than the point to be decided in court was whose blood was nearer the original stock. The party so favored by the decision was thus entitled to the inheritance. This grand assize, or royal court, thus allowed disputing parties to contest their civil rights without fear of life or limb. The grand assize had been originated at the Council of Windsor in 1179.[48]

In the actual workings of the grand assize there appears for the first known time the concept of challenging a juror. After the defendant had elected the assize, the plaintiff, upon appearing at the court swore a writ allowing four knights of the shire (county) to elect twelve other knights who were to hear and determine the dispute. The four knights charged with selecting the jury of twelve, did so in open court, and the defendant was allowed three "essoins," or challenges, against any of the twelve jurors selected. If the defendant appeared not in court on the day of jury selection, tradition, not the law, pressured those charged with jury selection to choose as many extra jurors as the defendants had "essoins." If on the day the four knights were to select a jury, less than four appeared, the absence number would be filled by others who were present that day at court, subject of course to the approval of the judge(s) and the advocating parties. To avoid the above, however, it became the practice to select and call two alternate knights to court for ensuring that four would be available.[49]

The twelve jurors would, on the day so appointed, be charged upon their oaths to hear and observe all witnesses and evidence presented by the advocating parties, and subsequently, to decide the suit.[50] If in the course of their deliberations, however, the jury found itself unable to deliver a unanimous verdict, extra jurors were added until there were twelve who agreed on a decision. An appeal from a decision of the grand assize could only be made to the king himself.[51]

In the case of criminal judicial proceedings the accused was either confined or retained in the local area by means of sureties (bonds) held by the court. In the case of a homicide charge confinement was mandatory. An investigation was conducted by the county sheriff, and all circumstances and evidence, previous record, the reputation of the accused—even conjectures—were carefully considered. The accused, upon conviction by the jury, or prior to the trial if he so elected, could absolve himself of all guilt by the "ordeal of water." However, if said ordeal substantiated a verdict of guilty and the accused survived—provided his offense was a felony—then he was subject to loss of life or members at the king's mercy. As previously mentioned there was a growing skepticism as to the reliability of the ordeal. This doubt is reflected in the penalty for failure to prove innocence by the trial of ordeal: "...at the king's mercy." Previously, tradition and law required the loss of one or the other—no mercy was allowed.[52]

On the day of jury selection for the criminal trial, the same right of "essoins" were allowed. When the jury selection process had been completed, the accuser was required to present his charges, and state that he was prepared to present witnesses and other evidence to prove his charges.[53] Although the records are not completely clear on this next point, it appears that if the evidence against the accused was less than conclusive, the issue was referred to the perils of trial by battle.[54]

When a subject of the realm found himself accused of the theft of precious metals (a probable reference to coins and other manmade objects), the procedure was as mentioned previously. However, if the charge was based only on the public infamy of the accused, he was not required to purge himself by the ordeal prior to conviction by the court. If found guilty, he could escape punishment only by undergoing the trial of ordeal. The same procedure applied to homicide, except that the accuser had to be of the same blood as the victim of the crime. In crimes involving arson, robbery, rape, and thefts other than precious metals, there was an additional requirement. The victim was required to appear at the nearest village to the scene of the crime, declare the crime and exhibit any physical evidence, then repeat the process before the court of the hundred (reive), and lastly in the county court (shire).[56]

Toward the end of his reign King Henry II established a group of five judges to hear cases designated "clamores hominum"—which is translated as "common pleas." It is alleged that this group did not constitute a new supreme court, but was designed to follow the king around the realm and bring about a closer relationship between the throne and the local courts. This was necessitated by the failure of the six circuit courts which covered the kingdom (three judges per court) to accomplish the king's wish for speedy justice. The five judges, as part of the king's

FIGURE 6: COURT SYSTEM OF 12TH CENTURY ENGLAND

Although variations occurred from time to time, this judicial structure is a fairly accurate representation of the English court system toward the close of the 12th century, and near the end of the reign of King Henry II.

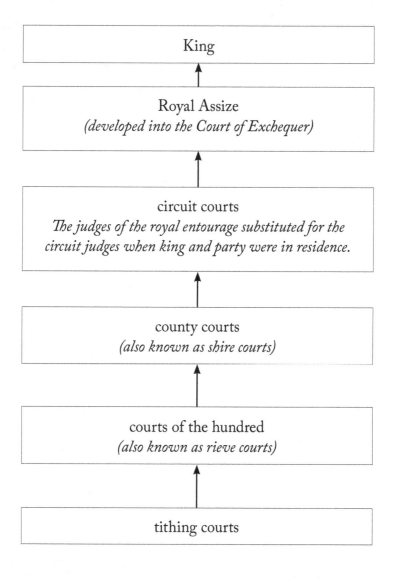

King

Royal Assize
(developed into the Court of Exchequer)

circuit courts
The judges of the royal entourage substituted for the circuit judges when king and party were in residence.

county courts
(also known as shire courts)

courts of the hundred
(also known as rieve courts)

tithing courts

entourage, were to sit in place of the judges of the local court wherein the king was residing. If they were unable to decide a case, or the party adversely effected by a judicial decision desired to appeal, the matter was immediately referred to the king for his decision.[56]

The reign of King Henry II was important in the development of professional judges, in the use of the royal assize, in the subjection of more and more law to the interpretation of the royal court (thus the same law for all), and, in the common usage of jury trials. In fact, it was implied that the common use of juries during King Henry's reign had its roots in the pre-Norman period, that in fact it may have had its origin in Danelaw—that part of mid-eastern England which was for years ruled by the Danes. Thus, without question, the rule of Henry II has to be regarded as the most important milestone in the history of early English judicial development.[57]

CHAPTER TWO

Colonial Jurisprudence in Virginia and Massachusetts, 1607–1661

The colonists who came to the shores of America in the early years of the 17th century were emphatic about retaining their "rights as Englishmen"—and the charters under which they established their new homes guaranteed these rights. Included in the list were, freedom from arrest and imprisonment except on specific charges, due process of law, and trial by jury. The settlers had been directly affected by the religious turmoil of 16th and 17th century England, in as much as it was the motivating force (plus economics in the case of Virginia) which caused many of them to sever their roots of country and home, to brave the dangers of the North Atlantic, and to start a new life on the edge of an immense primeval wilderness.

It was this strong religious conviction, interwoven with a natural tendency to imitate the states of the Old World, that established the theocratic governments of Virginia, New Plymouth, and Massachusetts Bay. Thus the first settlements of English settlers in North America believed in the unity of church and state, and (with the exception of New Plymouth) in the prosecution of religious dissenters. Their leaders acquiesced in a limited form of democracy, only, because the environment necessitated everyone's cooperation. Democracy was actually their foe.[1]

The first charter of King James I for the two colonies of Virginia—of which New Plymouth was to have been the second colony—bears the date of April 10, 1601. The first enduring settlement in Virginia called James City in honor of the king, was established on April 26, 1607.[2] The charter for these colonies was set forth by King James I in letters to Sir Thomas Gates, Sir George Somers, and other investors interested in sponsoring colonizing efforts. Each colony, wrote the King, is to have a council of thirteen members to act as the executive and judicial body for enforcing the laws and hearing all cases involving disputes and violations of said laws. The legislative branch shall be the Superior Council of Thirteen which shall be headquartered in London, England.[3] No laws, however, shall be enacted which would deprive any colonial subject, or children thereof, of any of the privileges of British subjects.[4]

The Virginia Company's Supreme Council (believed to have been the company's executive council sitting in London) was to nominate the members of the first council to be established in each of the colonies, with the members thereof, selecting their own president.[5] And then the charter proceeded to describe the judicial procedures to be followed in the colonies in the following manner:

> ...and that the said several presidents and councells, and the greater number of them within every of the several limits and precints, shall have full power and authority, to hear and determine all and every one of the offenses aforesaid, within the precints of their several

colonies, in the manner and forme following, that is to say, by twelve honest and indifferent persons sworne upon the Evangelist, to be returned by such ministers and officers as every of the said presidents and councells, of the most part them respectively shall assigns, and the twelve persons see returned and sworne shall, according to their evidence to be given unto them upon oath and according to the truth, in their conscience, either convict or acquit every of the said persons soe to be accused and tried by them....[7]

The company president and council, sitting in England, shall establish all courts that are needed in each of the respective colonies. So spoke the king in the first charter.[8] The second charter, enacted by the king in May 1609, restated the previous judicial instructions with no additions.

The third charter, however, which was issued in March 1611–2,[9] called for the establishment of a general court in the Colonies of Virginia, with sessions to be held four times a year. This assembly, to be entitled the "Four Great and General Courts of the Council and Company of Adventurers for Virginia," was charged with electing the members of the governor's council and such other officials as they decided were necessary to make and enforce the laws.[10] This same charter authorized the Virginia Company to cause the arrest of all persons believed to be guilty of committing crimes in the colonies, and either transport them for trial in England by the aforementioned company authorities, or if circumstances so dictated, to place them on trial before the colony council. From the beginning of the settlement in 1607 to 1621, when the 3rd legislative assembly was held—the first was held in 1619—this was the procedure utilized by the settlers at James City.[11]

It was from these first legislative assemblies that a formal governmental structure finally emerged. Henceforth there was to be a Council of State to assist and advise the governor of the colony; the members thereof to be elected from time to time by the Treasurer and company council seated in London, England. Another body was to be the General assembly, which was to consist of two burgesses from each town and plantation together with the Council of State. Its laws were to be subject to the governor's veto power, and ratified by the General Assembly in March 1623–4, a formal court system was erected within the Colony of Virginia. This consisted simply of two monthly courts, one to be held in James City and the other in Elizabeth City, with jurisdiction over all cases not exceeding 100 lbs. tobacco, plus misdemeanors. The judges were to be appointed by the Council of "State." All appeals from decision of the monthly courts were to be heard by the said council. If on completion of an appeal hearing the original verdict was upheld, the appellant was to be assessed double damages and fines in all civil cases.[13] At this stage in the judicial development of Virginia, the juries were not necessarily comprised of twelve men, there sometimes being more or less, considering cases within a few days of each other.[14]

In February of 1631–2, upon the establishment of counties, the General Assembly created four more monthly Courts. Each monthly court was to hear only cases originating within its boundaries. The justices, referred to as commissioners— later changed to justices of the peace—continued to hold the same jurisdiction over all misdemeanors and small civil matters.[15]

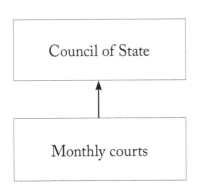

FIGURE 7: COURT SYSTEM OF COLONY OF VIRGINIA, 1624

During the next decade the assembly established the

Figure 8: Court System of Colony of Virginia, 1642

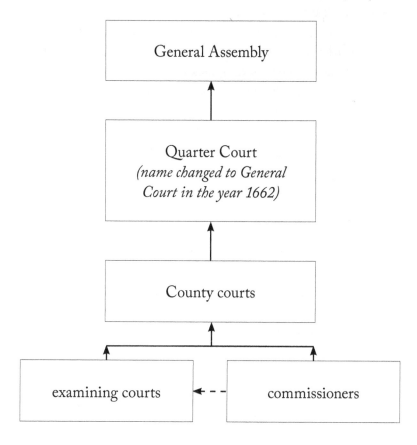

Quarter Court; so called, because it met in session four times a year. This court was placed in the judicial structure just below the General Assembly, which now became the court of last resort. The court's composition was to be the council of State, but, by another name. The Quarter Court was to exercise original jurisdiction in all felony cases, and in all civil suit where the value exceeded 500 lbs. tobacco, or the value thereof; and, to exercise appellate jurisdiction over all appeals from the monthly courts. If upon appeal to the Quarter Court, the original verdict was upheld, the appellant, provided he sought no higher appeal, was liable for double the original assessment of damages and fines. If, however, he carried his appeal to the General Assembly and the original verdict was still upheld, he was then liable for triple the original assessment of damages and fines.[16]

At the 1642 sessions of the General Assembly it was enacted that all civil cases under the sum of 1,600 lbs. tobacco, or the value thereof, should be tried in the monthly courts; that said courts were to be called county courts thereafter, and were to change the frequency of their sessions to once every two months. Furthermore, that the justices of these courts were to be entitled commissioners of the county courts. The total number of commissioners of any county, as a group, were to constitute the bench of the appropriate county court. It was during this same year that the commissioners were given jurisdiction to hear minor civil and criminal cases as individual justices. Later on these commissioners of the county courts started to meet once a month as sort of "examining courts" to determine which felony cases (which had come to their attention through the office of a single commissioner) should be referred to the county courts for trial.

In order to relieve men of little means from financial harassment and ruination for petty and trivial debts, it was enacted that all civil cases under the value of twenty shillings, or 2 lbs. tobacco, would be placed under the jurisdiction of the nearest commissioner to the disputing parties. The commissioner's decision was to be final, as the assembly had declared that no court had the jurisdiction to be cognizance of said matters under any circumstances. And where there was noncompliance with the commissioner's decision, that justice was authorized to cast the culprit into jail.[17]

The attorneys of the Virginia Colony also came under the critical eye of the General Assembly at their sessions of 1642. For the first time, regulations, encased with the formality and power of the law, were established to ensure uniformity and eliminate the financial abuse which many members of the profession were substantiating by their exorbitant fees and practices. Henceforth, all attorneys were to be licensed by the courts wherein they pleaded their cases. Any attorney not licensed, could plead a case only with the expressed permission of the court which was to hear the case. Furthermore, no attorney could hold a license from more than two trial courts: the Quarter Court, and one county court; and his fee for pleading a case in a county court was to be limited to 20 lbs. tobacco, or the value thereof, and in the Quarter Court, to 50 lbs. tobacco, or the value thereof. Violations were to be subjected to fines of 500 lbs. tobacco in the county courts, and 2,000 lbs. tobacco in the Quarter Court. In addition, it was to be prohibited in the future for any attorney to refuse his professional services to anyone, unless the other party to any dispute had already secured his services.[18]

In 1645 the county courts were given jurisdiction in all cases at common law, both civil and criminal, plus equity. This was deemed necessary because of the great distance of many areas of the colony from the capital in James City, the slow and laborious traveling conditions, and the dangers to be encountered from man, beast, and weather. All juries were ordered to be impaneled by the county sheriff, and there was to be a jury for all cases heard—if demanded by either the plaintiff or the defendant. And in each jury trial the said jurors were to be kept from food and drink until they had reached a unanimous verdict. It was not entirely clear, but the prosecutor in criminal cases throughout 17th century Virginia was apparently either the sheriff or an ordinary citizen bringing charges—following the custom of the mother country.

This same General Assembly said all suits in chancery were to be initiated by the following procedure. Any citizen who claimed cause of equity was required to request the issuance of a summons from one of the commissioners of the county court. The resulting subpoena, issued by the clerk of the court and signed by the commissioner, ordered the appearance of the defendant party to appear in court upon a certain date. If it was required that a deposition be taken, the same had to be conducted in court before two commissioners with the plaintiff and defendant present—or their attorneys on their behalf. It was further ordered during this session, that for the lessening of court business and the expense and trouble of the citizenry, that any defendant in such an aforementioned suit, could answer said subpoena by acknowledging the debt to the complaining party in writing; and that upon presentation to the clerk of the court, this written admission became as legally binding as if decreed— by the court in session.[19]

The first recorded appearance in Virginia of the grand jury as a judicial instrument occurred toward the end of 1645. It was declared by the legislature that during the month of March, and again in the middle of the summer, a grand jury was to be impaneled in each county to inquire into all violations of the criminal law not trespassing on those involving life and limb. The finding of each jury was to be reported to the local county court. The court was then required to take cognizance of said crimes by ordering the arrest and trial of the offenders, or, if of sufficient importance to more than one county, to be transferred to the Quarter Court. And in regard to the interaction between the county courts, the legislature issued a ruling: that any judgement of one county court was to be honored in the execution thereof by all other counties.[20]

In England a civil war had been fought between the Puritan Parliament and the king's forces, and had ended in the king losing his head. In 1652 the first meeting of the Virginia legislature occurred following a meeting of colonial leaders with the new English authorities. As a result of the aforementioned meeting, the General Assembly met in session with vastly enlarged powers over their previous authority. Their powers now included executive, legislative, and judicial combined.

Until the restoration of the monarchy occurred in 1660, the assembly elected the governor, and then elected the members of the Council of State, or, passed judgement on the governor's nominations. The assembly, now referred to as the "House of Burgesses," was not bound by any constitutional limitations, and consequently, dispensed and withdrew power as they considered necessary. Thus it was, that during this session the assembly commenced the practice of selecting the commissioners of the various counties in the colony.[21]

In March of 1655 that portion of the act of 1645 which had authorized the county courts to try all criminal cases was repealed. The House of Burgesses made it quite clear that the dispensation of justice in criminal matters involving life and limb had frequently been subjected to abuse; that impartiality and caution in dealing with alleged offenders was found lacking in the county courts. Therefore, it was ordered that all such future cases, including those presently in the judicial system, were to be transferred to the jurisdiction of the Quarter Court. In civil cases, the verdict of the county courts in all disputes less than 1,600 lbs. tobacco was to be final. If over 1,600 lbs. tobacco, then an appeal could legally be considered by the Quarter Court. Such an appeal, however, required the posting of a security bond; and if the verdict was upheld on appeal, the bond was to be forfeited as compensation to the court.[22]

The method of selecting the commissioners of the counties was again handed to the Council of State; but, with the modification that the candidates had to be acceptable to the other county commissioners.[23] It was further ordered that a single commissioner was to have jurisdiction in all civil cases not exceeding the value of a hogshead of tobacco set at 350 lbs.; that two commissioners were to have jurisdiction in all cases not exceeding the value of three hogsheads of tobacco set at 1,000 lbs. If the party adversely effected in any case judged by two commissioners (no appeal from the decision of one) appealed to the county court, any commissioner who had been involved in the original decision was prohibited from the appeal.

In March of 1657 the Virginia Assembly decided on a compensation bill for all jurors. They declared that in any legal dispute, the party who first demanded a jury trial, whether the plaintiff or the defended, would be required to pay 72 lbs. tobacco to the jurors. The legislature failed to clarify the point, but it is believed that the above amount was to be divided; not paid to each individual juror. The act was very specific, however, that while the jury was debating the dispute neither party was to be allowed access to the jurors.[25] In addition, the authority for impaneling county grand juries was repealed on the grounds that success had been lacking in considerable detection of law violators; sheriffs, under-sheriffs, and clerks of the courts were forbidden to act as an attorney for any party in any court which normally utilized the services of his office; and, the Quarter Court (commonly known now as the General Court) was reduced from four sessions a year to three.[26]

Three years later in March of 1660/61 the number of commissioners was limited to eight in each county. The legislature felt that the excessive numbers had lent themselves to disputes among the justices, and as a consequence, had rendered their judicial decisions contemptible in the eyes of the citizens. It was also decided that the office of sheriff should be rotated among the commissioners, starting with the most junior member. Reimbursement was also declared as justified for witnesses attending court, with the rate to be set at 20 lbs. tobacco for each day required for travel to and from court, and 40 lbs. tobacco for each day in attendance until their testimony had been delivered. Non-appearance, however, would result in a fine of 1,000 lbs. tobacco if pertaining to the Quarter Court, and 350 lbs. tobacco if the absence was from a county court. Although the legislature neglected to specify the party paying said witnesses, there was no indication of change to the previous requirement of each party to a dispute, paying for their own witnesses. And as before, each party to a dispute was limited to three witnesses on any point at issue.[27]

Before we continue any further in the development of the judicial system of colonial Virginia, an examination of the settlements to the north, New Plymouth and Massachusetts Bay, and their embryonic judicial systems is in order. A group of Puritan exiles from the Church of England, known as the Separatists, obtained a patent to found a colony in the northern part of what constituted the northern area of Virginia in the early 17th century: the mouth of the Hudson River. Following their sighting of Cape Code on November 9, 1620, severe weather conditions forced the weary travelers to establish their settlement on the nearby shores. Consequently, their patent was invalidated since they were outside the boundaries of the Virginia Colony. Therefore, on board the Mayflower they made a compact amongst themselves to serve as their basis of governmental authority. Known as the Mayflower Compact, it sworn each and every one into a body politic—agreeing to abide by all the laws which would be enacted thereafter.[28]

The Charter of the Colony of New Plymouth, although devoid of any authority outside the boundaries of Virginia, called for a General Council consisting of a governor and several assistants. This body was to constitute the executive, the legislative, and the judicial authority of the colony.[29] This embryo of governmental effort was enhanced in 1623 by the addition of the right to a jury trial for all offenders of the colony's laws. The law was written as follows:

> It was ordained 17 day of December An. 1623 by the court then held that all criminal facts, and also all maters of trespasses and debts betweene man and man should be tried by the verdict of twelve honest men to be impanelled by authority in forme of a jury upon their oath.[30]

In 1631 the colony experienced its first capital sentence in any judicial proceedings. That the judicial system had improved is illustrated by the fact that the offender, one John Billinton, was the first citizen on record to be indicted by a grand jury. Then at his trial before the General Council he was found guilty by the petit jury of the murder of one John Newcomin, and to quote Mr. John Bradford, Governor of the colony—"by plaine and notorious evidence."[31]

During this same year the General council enacted a law authorizing a juror to be reimbursed for jury duty: each member to receive six pences, except the foreman, who was to receive twelve pences. Although the law failed to specify who was to pay the jurors, the custom of the time would require the plaintiff or party demanding the jury in civil trials to shoulder the cost, and in criminal, either the defendant or the colony.

Five years later in 1636 a number of laws enhanced the governmental structure and procedures—including the judiciary. First to be enacted, was a law requiring that all elections should be held on the first Tuesday of March each year for the purpose of selecting all officers deemed necessary for the proper governing of the colony. Then in the following sequence, a requirement that the governor and his seven assistants would be elected for a period of one year; and that a treasurer (who could also be an assistant concurrently), a clerk of the court, and a coroner would also be elected for a similar period of time. The governor was to have a double vote in all matters which came within the cognizance of the council.[32] It was reiterated that the assistants were responsible for advising the governor in the execution of all the laws of the colony, to serve as judges of the court when the council held court for criminal trials and civil disputes, and, pending the governor's return when absent, to commit criminal offenders to jail.

When a colonial matter of considerable importance was at issue, either criminal or civil, the governor and his assistants—at their discretion—were charged with summoning all the freemen to appear at the General Council. The freemen of the colony, with the exception of the jurors and a few others, were to sit together with the council members as a General Court. This body was charged with both legislative and judicial responsibilities: to derive a law if legislative, or if a trial, to assess damages or possibly, to determine a criminal sentence. Regardless of the matter, it was decided by majority vote. Furthermore, it was mandatory that all freemen attend, and failure to heed the summons was punishable by a fine of three shillings.

During this same year it was declared that a grand jury must be impaneled by the governor and his assistants, or a majority thereof, to inquire into all breaches of the criminal law and present their findings to the General Council or General Court upon sworn oath. The oath was to be administered by an assistant. Where previously no one but the freemen of the colony could legally sit as jurors, it was now declared, that henceforth, status as a freeman (based on land ownership and membership in the established church of the colony) was not a necessary qualification for this duty. An additional power was given to the governor—whereas he was to be allowed, accompanied by two assistants, to hear all civil cases under forty shillings and all misdemeanors offenses.[33]

There was considerable complaint from the freemen of the colony about the requirement of attending the General Court,

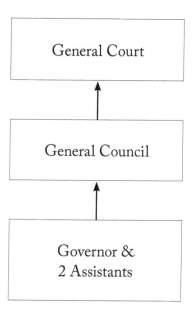

FIGURE 9: COURT SYSTEM OF NEW PLYMOUTH COLONY, 1645

so in 1637 the General Court, with all the freemen attending, modified the law so that two freemen would thereafter be elected to represent each village in the court. These representatives were to be entitled "Deputies of the General Court." In 1645, however, the complete exemption of freemen from the General Court was modified by the requirement that all freemen were required to attend the annual June session. At this session the names of the deputies who were to attend the other two sessions were to be announced, and then, this same session was to handle all of the legislative business of the colony for that year. The other two sessions, attended only by the General Council members and the deputies, were to be restricted to judicial matters only. Thus, after only twenty-five years in the wilderness, the Colony of New Plymouth had taken its first step toward a separation of the governmental powers.[34]

At this point in our narrative, we'll regress a few years in time to the beginning of the Massachusetts Bay Colony in 1630, and as in the case of Virginia, follow its judicial development through 1661. This is necessitated by the historical fact, that of the two northern colonies Massachusetts Bay quickly became the dominant settlement, and subsequently, in time, absorbed the older and smaller colony. This Calvinistic group of Puritans, some 1,000 in number and led by Governor John Winthrop, came ashore a few miles north of New Plymouth. Due to the fact that their charter failed to specify where the stockholders were to sit in council, the latter, as leaders of the group, simply moved the company headquarters to the new world.[35]

Their charter provided for a "great and general court," consisting of the governor, deputy governor, eighteen assistants, and as amended in practice, the freemen of the colony—who were required to own property, and to be members of the colony's established church. The requirements for church membership were very strict. This assembly was to meet four times a year, and had executive, legislative, and judicial authority.[36] Under the charter the right to a trial was established from the beginning of the settlement. Also an element of the judicial procedure as early as 1631, was the use of a grand jury to inquire into possible violations of the criminal law.[37]

In 1634 the composition of the Great and General Court was changed to exclude the freemen, except for two elected deputies from each village, for three of the four annual sessions. These three sessions were for the

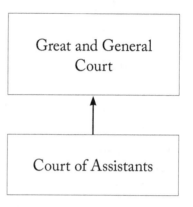

FIGURE 10: COURT SYSTEM OF MASSACHUSETTS BAY COLONY, 1634

Great and General Court

Court of Assistants

purpose of revising and repealing laws, and, to recommend new ones to the newly created Court of Assistants: the judicial role of the legislative colonial assembly. Then at the fourth annual session of the Great and General Court all freemen were to attend for the sole purpose of selecting all of the aforementioned governmental officials. Then in late 1634 the recently enacted law allowing only the court of assistants to make new laws was repealed, and that function was granted to the three annual Great and General Courts attended only by the deputies and the members of the Court of Assistants. Anyone accused of a crime was to be tried before this court.[38]

Definite procedures were created in 1634 for selecting and summoning men for jury duty. Prior to the sitting of each court session, the clerk thereof was to forward warrants to each town, in direct proportion to its population, requiring the constable to notify the freemen that election of jurors for the forthcoming court was now required. All jurors were to be compensated at the rate of four shillings a day. The statue failed to specify the party, or parties, responsible for such compensation; but the custom of the time indicates that it was not the colony except in cases of indigent offenders. If the court in question was the Court of Assistants, which met in the capital of the colony at Boston, then for the sake of individual convenience, the jurors were drawn only from the immediate surrounding counties. The jurors were expressly directed to be the trier of facts, and the judges to interpret and instruct the jury as to the meaning of the law.[39] If a case involved a matter of equity such as the forfeiture of an obligation or the violation of a covenant without damages, the court was to decide the issue. A trial by jury, specifically selected for that purpose, was declared mandatory in every case involving possible loss of life or banishment. In addition to the petit juries, a grand jury, selected in the same manner as aforementioned, was to be summoned unto every court session to inquire into all alleged violations of the criminal law, and subsequently, to present their findings to the court. This jury was not required to reveal to the court those crimes, which in the opinion of majority members presented no danger to the colony or any member thereof. The rate of compensation, to be paid by the colony to members of grand juries, was set at three shillings a day.[40] No juror, it was decided, shall be required to serve on any other jury during that calendar year; except, if he had been selected for grand jury duty, or where his services were needed in cases involving life and death, or banishment.[41]

In a very unique decision of the legislators, it was enacted in 1634 that petite juries could present a "Special Verdict" to the court in all cases where they were unable to decide on the exact meaning of the law. Instead of submitting their question of interpretation back to the court and then proceeding accordingly, the jury was authorized to return a double-edged verdict, to wit:

If the law means such and such, we find for the plaintiff—but, if it means thus and that we find for the defendant.

Thus, the court, as the interpreter of the law, was responsible for the selection of the appropriate verdict. If the court and a jury, where a single verdict had been returned, should disagree on the determination, then the issue was to be continued until the next Court of Assistants. During the next year it was decided that if a judge was related by blood or marriage, or enjoyed a friendship with either party to a case before him, that he was disqualified from deciding the case.[42]

In 1635, and then again two years later in 1637, the Great and General Court had occasion to sit in judgement of a religious dissenter: first, Roger Williams, and secondly, Anne Hutchinson.[43] In each case the accused stood at one end of a long table, the governor seated at the other end with the deputy governor and assistants, plus deputies, seated on either side. With the governor acting as chief justice, witnesses and evidence were brought before the court. Since the role of a public prosecutor was still many years from being a part of the judiciary system, the role of the magistrates was a combined one of judge and prosecutor. The accused was required to conduct his, or her, own defense. Although the right to a jury trial was supposedly guaranteed, there is no evidence that such was allowed in the trials of these religious dissenters from the Puritan (Congregational) faith.[44] Both Williams and Hutchinson were convicted and sentenced to serve the religious punishment of banishment from the colony. As a consequence of so many civil offenses being considered within the purview of religion, the courts of Massachusetts Bay Colony were both secular and religious courts of law. Usually the offender's church congregation also took punitive action against the individual; the most drastic penalty being excommunication of a member.[45]

In the year 1639, restructuring of the court system resulted in the addition of three purely judicial elements: the creation of the inferior quarter courts (forerunner of the county courts), the office of commissioners (later known as the justices of the peace), and the authorization of a judicial hearing by a single magistrate (assistant). At the apex of the judicial structure was the great and General Court; then in descending order, the Court of Assistants, the inferior quarter courts, the individual magistrates (deputies), and in villages where no deputy resided, a commissioner. The Great and General Court, as the only judicial body established by the colony's charter, exercised both original and appellate jurisdiction in civil, religious, and criminal matters.[46] The Court of Assistants (also referred to as the Great Quarter Court) held sessions four times a year until 1649; then, its sessions were reduced to two. This court was given original jurisdiction in all criminal cases involving life and limb, and those of banishment. Later, they were also given cognizance of all divorce cases. In civil disputes they were authorized jurisdiction whenever the value exceeded 10 lbs. The court also had appellate jurisdiction over the inferior quarterly courts, plus the single actions of magistrates and commissioners.[47]

The inferior quarter courts (county courts), originally four in number, met four times a year. Their jurisdiction extended over all civil disputes where the value did not exceed 10 lbs., and all criminal cases not involving life and member, or banishment, and later on, divorce and probate cases. The composition of this type court, of three to five members, was one assistant, with the remainder being commissioners who were elected by the freemen of the county.[48]

During either 1638 or 1639 limited jurisdiction was extended to single magistrates (assistants) which allowed such an official to hear non-jury cases not exceeding twenty shillings in value. Appeals were directly to the Court of Assistants, since the inferior quarterly courts had concurrent jurisdiction.[49]

In response to the desires of the citizenry, the Great and General Court, in 1641, enacted a code of laws to guide and restrain the magistrates in the exercise of their discretion, and consequently, protect the rights of the people. Entitled the "Body of Liberties," the unprecedented step was taken of submitting the code to the people of each village for their personal ratification. The code was enacted in the following manner:

> It is therefore ordered by this court and the authority thereof, that no man's life shall be taken away, no man's honour or good name shall be tainted, no man's person shall be arrested, restrained, banished, dismembered, no ways punished; no man shall be deprived of his wife or children, no man's goods or estate shall be taken away from him, nor any ways damaged, under colour of law, or countenance of Authority, unless it be by virtue or equity of some expressed law of the country warranting same, established by a General Court, and sufficiently published; or in case of the desert of a law, in any particular case, by the word of God. And in capital cases, or in any cases concerning dismemberence, or banishment, according to that word, to be judged by the General Court.[50]

The following laws, which were enacted during the year of 1641, helped to provide substance to the "Body of Liberties." The first law enacted, declared that any individual who brought suit against another, for whatever the reason, would upon the facts being known by the court, pay to the defendant triple the damages otherwise assessed in a suit which had failed of proof; and, furthermore, was to pay a fine of forty shillings to the court.[51] A grand jury of twelve men, it was decided, would be called whenever an assistant, or a village constable, suspected that a death was untimely and due to unnatural causes. If such was then substantiated, the evidence would be presented to an assistant or to the next inferior quarter court.[52] Any person charged with a crime or as a party to a civil dispute, it was enacted, shall have the right to either a bench or jury trial. If a jury trial was selected, in any case whatsoever, both advocates were to possess the right to challenge any juror for cause, and either the bench or the remainder of the jury, as decided by the party challenging, shall decide if the bias for the challenge is to be allowed. This right was declared as mandatory regardless of the age or mental condition, stranger or resident.[53] And also, no individual could be executed for any capital offense without the sworn testimony of two witnesses, or, by other evidence which would be the equivalent.[54]

During the following year all cases of civil disputes were ordered to commence their legal action through a magistrate, commissioner, or the local inferior quarterly court.[55] In order to prevent frivolous civil suits the plaintiff in each and every suit was to pay a fee of ten shillings upon filing, unless the court allowed suit pasperis (paupers); and, if said plaintiff should fail in his suit he was to pay all court cost. In reference to appealing a case, any party adversely affected by the judicial decision of a commissioner, a magistrate, or an inferior quarterly court, could hereafter appeal to the Court of Assistants. Such an appeal required the posting of a security bond: in civil cases to pay for damages and court cost if the original decision was upheld; and, in criminal, to ensure the appearance of the defendant. In capital cases if two of every five assistants on the court differed in their opinion as to the merit of the appeal, then the appellant could take his appeal to the next session of the Great and General Court convened for hearing judicial matters. It was further enacted that a judge of an inferior court was prohibited from hearing an appeal on the same case; nor, could any appellant court consider any evidence not presented during the trial.[56]

The assembly of Massachusetts Bay, in 1647, ruled that any magistrate or commissioner could depose any witness, fourteen years or older, who lived more than ten miles from court, and thereafter be required to present the deposition in court or to a public notary to be recorded. This was applicable in both civil and

FIGURE 11: COURT SYSTEM OF MASSACHUSETTS BAY COLONY, 1647

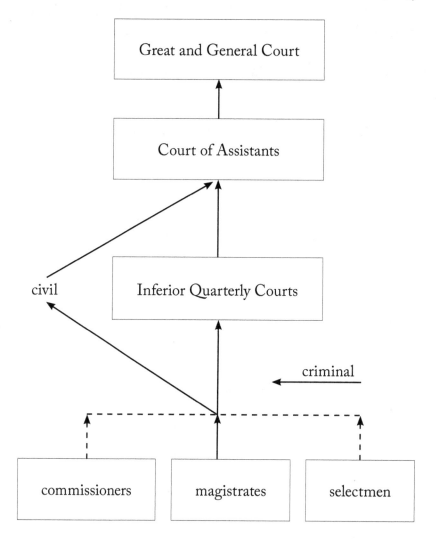

criminal cases; except among the latter, those cases of a capital nature. Parties to a civil suit were ordered by the legislature to henceforth pay their witnesses two shillings a day for travel to and from court; unless the distance was less than three miles, then the reimbursement was limited to six pences a day. Attendance

Figure 12: Court System of Massachusetts Bay Colony, 1660

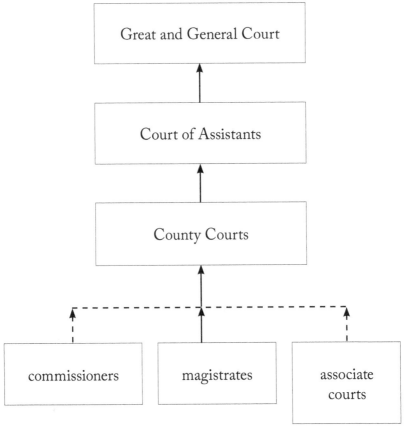

(Selectmen still substituted for commissioners and magistrates as enacted by the legislature of 1647.)

at court was to be reimbursed by the authorities.[57] It was further enacted that in those small communities, where a magistrate or commissioner might be personally involved in a civil matter of small value, a substitute official, known as a selectman, was to hear the matter in dispute.[58]

Four years later, in 1651, the precedence was established in Boston that any five commissioners, or three plus a magistrate (assistant), could hear a civil matter of a value not to exceed 10 lbs. This action had been necessary to relieve the case load on the inferior quarterly courts. The aforementioned was referred to as associate courts. The inferior quarterly courts, now referred to as the county courts, were around this period of time stripped of their concurrent jurisdiction with single magistrates, commissioners, and associate courts. Instead, they became the immediate courts of appeal for such judicial decisions.[59] Then in 1660 the Court of Assistants lost all original jurisdiction, becoming strictly an appellate court in the judicial system of Massachusetts. Its original criminal jurisdiction was assumed by the Great and General Court, and its civil jurisdiction by the county courts.[60]

CHAPTER THREE

Colonial Jurisprudence in Virginia, 1661–1775

At the start of the above noted period, both of the colonies of Massachusetts[1] and Virginia[2] had established well defined court systems and judicial procedures. Both were products of the Puritan 16th and 17th century upheaval in England, in that they came to the shores of the New World as the initial migrating wave of reaction to the disrupting religious struggle. In the case of the Massachusetts colonies, it was primarily a religious reaction, in that they had turned from the task of destroying the heretical elements within the Church of England to the task of erecting the true religious community in a world far removed from the tainted existence of the Old World. In the case of Virginia, however, it was primarily as a reflection of the economics of capitalism, which, in its struggle with the ancient concept of feudalism, formed the central core and foundation of the English religious turmoil. Reactions to religious aspects of the turmoil in England were thus secondary factors in motivating the majority of the settlers who came to Virginia.[3]

Not only were the settlers of Virginia less extreme in their Puritan beliefs than those who settled further north, but subsequently, after 1660, Puritanism was gradually diluted and eliminated as a major factor of life by the successful encroachment of the English feudalistic philosophy of life. Engineered by the royal governor, Governor Berkeley, it became the social, economic and judicial foundation of what became known as the "ante-bellum south." But regardless, the basic judicial structure, procedures, and legal rights, as established by the Virginian Puritans continued to survive and prosper.[4]

Picking up the theme of Virginian jurisprudence once more, we'll follow it through to the eve of the American Revolution. During the March 1662 session of the legislature, it was enacted that church wardens were to make a written presentment twice a year to the county courts concerning offenders of swearing, profaning God's holy name, abusing the Sabbath, drunkenness, fornication, adultery, etc.; and, that they were to be empowered to cause all such individuals to appear at the next session of these courts. Thus was the power of state religion further enhanced in colonial Virginia.

The Quarter Court, which had been reduced from four to three sessions some time previously, was given a new name: that of "General Court."[5] Because of the lack of procedural rules and the disorganization in the judicial proceedings of the general court, the following rules were declared to be mandatory in an attempt to correct this deficiency. First of all, the court was to be identified and declared in session by the cryer—then, the following ritual was to be followed.

Cryer: O yes, O yes, O yes, silence is commanded in the court while his Majesties _____ are sitting, upon paine of imprisonment.

Cryer: All manner of persons that have anything to doe at this court draw neer and give your attendance and if anyone have any plaint to enter or suite to prosecute lett them come forth and they shall be heard.

Cryer: Calling the plaintiff, _____, come forth and prosecute the action against the defendant, _____, or else thou will be non-suit.

Cryer: (if the plaintiff has appeared) calling the defendant. _____ come forth and save thy boyles or else thou wilt forefeit they recognizance.[6]

The 1662 Virginia legislature, although desiring to abide as close as possible to the laws and judicial procedures of England, was forced by circumstances unknown in the mother country to make certain concessions to the environment. Such was the situation they believed, with the selection of jurors for criminal trials in the General Court. The remoteness and dispersement of the habitations often made it difficult to draw all of the jurors from the area where a crime was committed. Therefore, it was declared that six of the jurors were to be selected from the area where the crime was committed, in order that they could acquaint the remaining jurors—picked from the bystanders— with the facts of the case. Jurors for this court were to be paid 20 lbs. tobacco a day for travel to and from, and while in attendance, 50 lbs. tobacco a day.[7]

Because of the delays that appeals to the General Court and the General Assembly were in the past subjected to; and the distance, expense, and dangers, to which the citizens were exposed, the 1662 legislature decided that any party adversely affected by a county court decision could appeal directly to the nearest two members of the General Court. If one of the justices was the governor himself, and appeal from this decision was desired, it was to be directed to the next General Assembly. Otherwise, the appeal was to the next General Court—minus the aforementioned commissioners.

Because courts are subject to error as frequently in small matters as large ones, the legislature resolved that no appeal would be denied because of small value or minute importance. However, all who appealed, must, as previously declared, post security for prosecution of the appeal and payment for damages if the suit be pronounced unjust. However, because the County of Northampton was so remote from the capital and the travel between the two so dangerous, no appeals were to be allowed from that County Court which were valued under 3,000 lbs. tobacco or 30 lbs. sterling.[8]

With the same thought of distance and danger in mind, it was declared that any witness whose testimony was required in a trial in General Court, and whose residence was some distance from the capital, or north of the York River, the clerk of the court would henceforth be required to issue a writ of dedimus potestatem for taking the deposition of said witness; except, in criminal trials, where their verbal testimony would still be required in court. In the taking of such depositions a member of the governor's council who resided in the same county as the witness, or any one of the county commissioners, were to be allowed to sign the writ for the taking of the deposition. Aside from the infrequent agreement of plaintiff and defendant as to three indifferent parties to conduct the deposition, the governor and council or any one of the county judges—the court not being in session—was to choose three citizens to conduct the deposition on a designated date and time; any two of the appointees being sufficient to execute the order of the law. Upon completion of said deposition, those so appointed—and who actually conducted the said proceedings—were to be required to sign and seal the testimony, and deliver the same to the clerk of either the local county court or the General Court.[9]

The title of the commissioners of the county courts was changed at this 1662 session to the one which was retained down to the present day: justices of the peace. And furthermore, it was enacted that any four of the justices constituted a quorum for a county court session.[10] And to enhance the aura of respect needed by all courts to ensure compliance with their decisions, it was ordered that the general court procedures for instilling such an atmosphere of respect be likewise enacted in the county courts. It was further ordered that these courts, in their jurisdiction, were prohibited from taking cognizance of any civil matter under 200 lbs. tobacco; such being deemed a matter for a justice of the peace.[11]

At this same legislative session some modifications were also made to the laws pertaining to juries. In reference to petit juries, previous laws had always decreed that such a right would be provided only if requested by one of the party to any case pending before a court. Now, the legislature, viewing such an arrangement as contrary to the laws of England, declared that every court in the colony was to have a jury impaneled by the county sheriff at the commencement of each day the court was in session. And that the jury was to hear all cases deemed proper by the court. Grand jury proceedings were reenacted after an absence of five years from the judicial proceedings of the colony, and required to meet thereafter in two sessions each year. Their duties were the same as before: to inquire into all possible violations of the criminal law and present their findings to the next county court.[12] Since previous incidences had apparently occurred where witnesses had refused to testify under oath, the legislature in late 1662, had ordered that all courts of the colony, plus the justices of the peace, were to have the authority to deal with such offenders by committing them to jail until they had sworn the oath and presented their testimony.

By 1677 the General Assembly had become aware that some of the justices of the peace were abusing the dignity of the county courts by appearing on the bench in various states of intoxication. Therefore, it was so ordered, that henceforth the following procedure would be utilized to deal with such deviating officials. That on the occasion of the first offense, as adjudged by his fellow justices of the county court, the justice would be fined 500 lbs. tobacco and caske; that for the second offense, 1,000 lbs. tobacco and caske; and, on the third occasion, 2,000 lbs. tobacco and cask, plus, removal from office and loss of commission.[14]

A forerunner of the 5th Amendment to our federal constitution was an answer provided by the General Assembly in October of 1677 to the Burgesses from Accomack County, Virginia.

> Upon a motion from Acomack County, sent by their Burgesses, it is answered and declared, that the law has provided that a person summoned as a witness against another ought to answere upon oath, but noe law can compell a man to sweare against himselfe in any matter wherein he is liable to corporall punishment.

A contrary development for the political and legal system of Virginia, was the enactment during the same year that two men from each parish, and four if a county in question had only one parish, were to sit with the justices of the county courts and have an equal vote in determination of sentences. Thus the theocratic society of colonial Virginia was provided with another knot of strength.[16]

During the last sixteen years of the 17th century there were laws implemented concerning court sessions, trials of slaves, failure of witnesses to appear for depositions, and the qualifications for being a juror. In 1684 the number of annual sessions of the General Court was reduced from three to two; to meet on the 15th of April and the 15th of October, for eighteen days on each occasion.[17] In 1692 it was believed that swift "justice" for slaves was required if the proper deterrence was to emanate from the courts. Therefore, it was enacted that any slave who had committed a violation of the law, was to be quickly arraigned and indicted, evidence taken upon the confession of the offender, two witnesses, or of one with pregnant circumstances, and the guilt or innocence then decided—all, without the right of a jury.[18] In 1696, due to the failure of some citizens to appear in response to a writ of dedimus potestatem for the taking of their testimony, it was enacted that a fine of 1,000 lbs. tobacco would be levied for failure to answer such a writ being issued from the General Court, and a fine of 350 lbs. tobacco when issued from a county court. However, the fine was to be revoked if the said citizen appeared at the next court session, and showed just cause why he had failed to answer the writ.[19] During the last year of the 17th century, 1699, property qualifications were established for all prospective jurors, varying in amount between the two types of courts. In the General Court a freeholder was to have property valued at 100 lbs. sterling, real or personal; and in the county courts, property valued at 50 lbs. sterling. This provision, naturally, disenfranchised a considerable number of citizens from the experience of jury duty.[20]

With the beginning of the 18th century a court of claims was established on the county level as part of the colony's judicial system. Entitled the court for proof of public claims, these courts were to meet in each county just prior to each session of the General Assembly, and hear all cases of colonial debt to private individuals. The claimant in each case was to produce the contract by which the government enlisted his services or purchased his products, to produce all business records and other evidence or testimony pertaining to proof of services rendered, and lack of compensation received. If the decision of the court favored the plaintiff, the contract and all evidence supporting the claim were to be carried by the county burgesses to the General Assembly for their approval of satisfaction of claim.[21]

The previous act for ensuring swift prosecution of slaves suspected of violating the criminal law was modified at this session in 1705. Authorization was given to the county sheriffs to select and appoint one freeholder of his choosing to assume responsibility for seeing that "justice" was done. This individual, who assumed the joint roles of investigator, prosecutor, judge and jury, upon determination that prosecution was warranted, had the offender publicly arraigned and indicted at the county courthouse. This special court then conducted the trial, and upon a determination of guilt, passed sentence with the full backing of the law. The only defense allotted the slave was the appearance of his master—if the latter chose to do so—to testify on the slave's behalf; but only in reference to the facts of the crime.[22]

The portion of the 1662 law which allowed witnesses in civil cases pending before the General Court to submit depositions in lieu of their personal testimony—provided that they resided at a remote location from the capital—was repealed during the aforementioned session of the general assembly. The 1705 act stated that all such witnesses, unless physically or mentally incapacitated, were required to attend and give their testimony in person. A certificate of disability, signed by a justice of the peace, had to be presented at court on behalf of any witness so designated. Thereon, the justices of the General Court, or any two of them, were to appoint such individuals as were required in accordance with established procedures for taking depositions, and instruct them to depose the witness at the latter's residence.

That tolerance was gradually seeping into Virginia's colonial society is illustrated by Act XXXI of the General Assembly of 1705. It states that although Catholics, negroes, Indians, and mulattoes, not being Christians, were incapable of being witnesses, Quakers were now to be allowed as competent witnesses in any Virginia court of law. The act further declared that the solemn affirmation and declaration of the Quakers was to be accepted in place of the usual oath required by the law.[23] Furthermore, it was enacted, witnesses shall be free from arrest, judgements, writs, or any other form of legal procedure not related to the case to which he has testimony of value. This immunity was to continue inviolate while traveling between his residence and the court, both going to and from, and while in attendance as a witness. In addition, a day's travel for a witness was set at twenty miles for a reimbursement of 1.5 lbs. tobacco per mile, plus toll charges incurred. While in attendance a witness was entitled to a fee of 60 lbs. a day. These witness fees were the responsibility of the party on whose behalf the witness was to testify.[24]

In reference to juries, the fall session of the 1705 legislature declared that county grand juries were to number twenty-four citizens of each county, and that such a jury for the general court was to be the same number from among the bystanders. Presentment of alleged offenses by grand juries was to be based on evidence of no less than two witnesses. In trials involving treason or felonies, the petit jury of the general court was to be selected in a manner different from that utilized for other offenses. The procedure was to commence with the issuance of a writ of venire facias to the sheriff of the county wherein the crime was committed. Upon receipt a selection was to be made of six freeholders who resided near the scene of the crime. Those so chosen were then instructed to appear at the next session of the court on the fourth day thereof. Any juror who so challenged was be replaced from amongst the bystanders. An additional six were to be selected from amongst the bystanders to complete the jury.[25]

In addition to the new courts of public claims, the legislature of 1705 saw a need for all communities to have municipal courts to handle civil matters under 30 lbs. sterling, and criminal cases involving petty offenses. This new court was to be called a court of hustings. Each community was to select eight men, twenty-one or older, to govern the village or town. Any three of these officials, to be called benchers, were to constitute the justices of each court of hustings. Court was to be held on a weekly basis.

All fines, none to exceed 5 lbs. sterling, were to be paid into the village treasury. Civil disputes exceeding 30 lbs. sterling were to be heard in the county courts; while any case on appeal was to be considered by the General court. The courts of hustings,[28] unlike the county courts and the General Court, were not to be courts of record.[29]

After the year of 1705, during which the capital buildings in James City were consumed by fire, the general assembly met in session at the new capital in Williamsburg.[30] Here, in 1711, the legislature enacted a comprehensive bill pertaining to the probate of wills and administration. It was declared that the county courts were to have jurisdiction over all matters and disputes involving wills, and the right of administration of estate left by persons dying intestate.[31] Exceptions to the jurisdiction of the county courts were the estates valued at 50 lbs. sterling or more which were located in two or more counties. Then, the General Court was to assume jurisdiction.[32]

In April of 1718 an act was passed which established definite fees for attorneys—a periodic occurrence to ensure compatibility with the economics of the times. When pleading a case in General Court, an attorney was to be entitled to a fee of fifty shillings, or 500 lbs. tobacco; and in a county court, fifteen shillings, or 150 lbs. tobacco. And, if upon settlement of a civil suit, the court in declaring against the defendant found that he had delayed the resolution for an unjustified reason; or, if upon declaring against the plaintiff, found that he had brought an unjustified suit, the court would fine the subject in question one attorney's fee to be paid to the opposing party. This fine was to be in addition to whatever damages might be awarded.[33]

Whenever the sheriff of a county serves a summons to appear in a civil suit, declared the legislature in 1727, and the said writ mentions no specific debt, nor any reference to bail, the said official is empowered to accept the signature thereon of any reputable attorney that he will appear in court on behalf of

FIGURE 13: COURT SYSTEM OF THE COLONY OF VIRGINIA, 1705

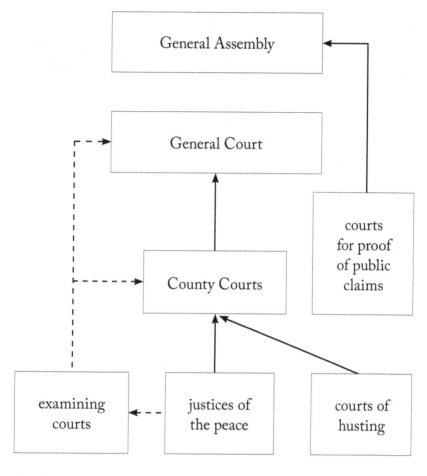

(See footnotes #26 and 27 this chapter, plus footnote #5, chapter five.)

the defendant at the assigned date and time.[34] And, whenever a defendant in custody awaiting trial lacks sufficient bail, pledges on his word that he will appear in court on the appointed day, and such pledge is accepted by the plaintiff, he may be released on his own recognizance. Although it could not be ascertained factually, the statute left no doubt that bail and imprisonment for the lack thereof, were as applicable to civil disputes as to criminal offenses.[35] In continuation of the above, the plaintiff could obtain an attachment, declared the legislature, against the defendant's estate to ensure his appearance. Subsequently, if the trial resulted in the non-appearance of the defendant, the plaintiff could recover his whole debt upon the filing of his attachment.[36] In addition, upon the non-appearance of the defendant, the plaintiff could request and have issued a writ to show cause to be served on the defendant. If the writ was returned non est inventus the plaintiff was entitled to request and have it declared by the court, that the defendant was outside the law.[37]

In May of 1730 a legislative bill was made into law by which the county courts, upon information of law violations filed by a sheriff or constable, shall instruct the prosecuting attorney to bring charges against the alleged offenders.[38] At the same session the assembly reinforced the ties of church and state, by stating that both church wardens and grand juries were authorized to file presentments of charges against anyone suspected of crimes against the Lord. All such persons were to be summoned to appear at the next General Court to answer the allegations. If convicted, punishment was to be denial of public office, of employment, or possibly imprisonment.[39]

Two years later it was decided that certain changes were required in the laws of evidence, and concerning the qualifications of attorneys practicing in the courts of Virginia. In May of that year it was ordered that the business records and private papers of a deceased person could be utilized in civil litigations concerning business disputes.[40] The only previous licensing requirement for attorney had been through the courts where they pleaded their cases, but the law had been ineffective; therefore, this 1732 legislature was determined to correct the judicial environment of unskilled and unscrupulous lawyers who infested the colonial courts of Virginia. It was therefore enacted, that no attorney in the colony was to practice law after the 10th of November, 1732, without a license issued by the governor and the Council of State. The procedure for obtaining said license was to start with a petition to the aforementioned council. This petition was to state the petitioner's qualifications and his request for the issuing of a license to practice law in the Colony of Virginia. Upon receipt of the petition the council was to nominate whatever individual(s) they deemed appropriate, known to be learned in the law, who would be charged with the responsibility of investigating the qualifications of the petitioner; and then, summarizing the findings with an accompanying recommendation to the council. If the recommendation was favorable to the petitioner, he would then be allowed to take the following oath in the presence of the council.

> You shall do no falsehood, nor consent to any to be done in court; and if you know of any to be done, you shall give notice thereof to the justices of the courts, that it may be reformed. You shall delay no man for lucre or malice, nor take any unreasonable fees. You shall not sittinly or willingly sue, or procure to be sued, any false suit, nor give aid nor consent to the same upon pain of being disabled to practice as an attorney forever. And furthermore, you shall use yourself in the office of an attorney within court according to your learning and discretion. So help you God.[41]

Several years later the General Assembly took up the situation of non-appearance of defendants at civil trial again. It was enacted that an affidavit was to be filed with the court in question, presumably by either the county sheriff or prosecutor (the latter had first appeared as a judicial officer in 1711), that the defendant is beyond the boundaries of the colony and is not to be located anywhere therein. Upon such a sworn statement the court was charged with issuing an injunction prohibiting the removal of the defendant's estate from the colony, and could at the same time, assign control of the estate to the plaintiff—pending, that is, a security bond being posted by the latter. The court was then to post notice for the defendant's appearance at the next court session, two months hence, in the Virginia Gayette, on the front floor of the capital, and by announcement at divine services. Such notification, it was ruled, would continue until the first day of the next court session. If at that time the defendant was still absent from the court, the suit was to be forfeited in favor of the plaintiff. And the estate, or that portion required to satisfy the judgement, would be awarded to the plaintiff.[42]

The first known instance in American jurisprudence where the court appointed counsel for a defendant possibly occurred in Virginia in the year of 1744. The Virginia legislature ruled that any defendant who refused to appear, and on being forced to so appear, refused to defend himself, to enter a plea, or to retain a lawyer of the court to act on his behalf, made it necessary for the court to take corrective action. This was to be accomplished by the court selecting a local attorney to enter a plea on behalf of the defendant, and to subsequently protect the latter's interest in all legal proceedings including trial. Although there is no evidence to suggest that such a service was provided without fee, this action on the part of the Virginia legislature was a significance development in the history of American jurisprudence.[43] During this same year, grand juries, in a departure from past practice, were placed under the restriction of a statute of limitation; that is, their presentment to the county courts were to be restricted to those offenses committed during the past year.[44]

Another judicial change occurred during 1744 in reference to the justices of the peace. And this was a change of major proportions. For the first time in over one hundred years, appeals from the decisions of the justices to the county courts was to be allowed. However, due notice was to be provided to the county prosecutor, and two sufficient bonds were to be posted with a justice of the peace—other than the one whose decision was being appealed.[45] At the same session it was enacted into law, that lack of proper procedures, or technical violations which occurred during criminal trials, were insufficient reason for the General Court to reverse a conviction where guilt was substantiated by the facts. And furthermore, in the future the court was instructed to ignore any appeal based on the aforementioned grounds.[46] In reference to who could testify as a witness, the General Assembly reflected the advancement of tolerance when they declared that Indians, free negroes, and mulattoes, could conceivably be Christians; and consequently, were qualified to be witnesses in any court of law—but—only against other Indians, negroes, and mulattoes—both free and slave.[47]

In 1753 the General Court was reaffirmed in their jurisdiction over all matters, civil, ecclesiastical, and criminal; by original jurisdiction in all civil disputes over 10 lbs. sterling, or 2,000 lbs. tobacco, plus all criminal cases of a capital nature; and appellate jurisdiction over all matter from inferior courts. The General Court, which met twice a year for sessions of twenty-four days, had set aside the first five days of each session to hear cases on appeal and certiorari, and the other nineteen days to hear cases of original jurisdiction.[48] One of the type cases which came within their jurisdiction was any matter, civil or criminal, involving a member of the Council of State. Since the council members also constituted the General Court, the member in question was automatically suspended until the legal termination of his case from all functions of the court.[49] Those civil cases not exceeding the 10 lbs., declared the legislature, could only be brought before the General Court in its appellate role when the matter involved title or boundaries of land. In all other cases of such value the decisions of the county courts were to be final.[50]

In this 1753 legislative assembly the process of removing cases from the inferior courts to the General Court by writ of certiorari was spelled out in detail. The party seeking a reversal of a trial court's unfavorable decision had to petition the Council of State for permission to have his case heard before the General Court—the court of last resort for the Colony of Virginia. In his petition the appellant was to state his reasons for believing that a hearing was necessary. Furthermore, he had to swear an oath before a magistrate as to the truth of the reasons previously stated. Upon termination of an appellate hearing granted on a writ of certiorari, the justices of the General Court could bring a charge of perjury against the appellant if they determined that the writ was based on allegations known by him to be false. If, however, twelve months elapsed without prosecution having commenced, the hapless defendant was to be free from any future attempt to prosecute the charge.[51]

The issue of habeas corpus was also before the General Assembly during the year of 1753, and the resulting law was enacted. If a prisoner of a county goal (jail) petitioned the General Court for a writ of habeas corpus, and the court determined that the offense was one over which they had jurisdiction, they were to issue said writ cum causa to remove the petitioner to the public jail in Williamsburg.[52] Henceforth, declared the assembly, all juries of the General Court, both grand and petit, were to be summoned by the county sheriff from among the local citizens living within a perimeter designated as a half a mile beyond the city limits of Williamsburg.[53]

Very little change took place within the judicial system of Virginia over the years subsequent to 1753, until the outbreak of the American Revolution. Then suddenly, in 1775, sometime between April and December of that year, the governor and his Council of State vanished as an entity of the government of the colony. And, since the aforementioned council also constituted the General Court, that judicial of last resort had also vanished. Subsequently, there must have been a period of weeks or months during which the judicial system ceased to operate as an

FIGURE 14: THE OPERATING COURT
SYSTEM OF VIRGINIA, 1775–1776

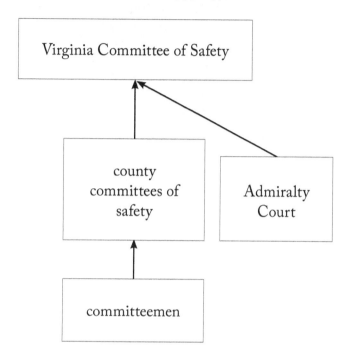

instrument of government. Then in December of that year the General Assembly appointed the colony's Committee of Safety to officially assume the duties of the governor and Council of State—and also to perform all the functions of the General Court The committee was also charged to appoint five individuals from among their members in each and every county, to act in place of the justices of the peace; both in the individual office, and in concert to act in place of the county court. It was decreed that all rights and judicial procedures were to remain in effect. There was no recorded provision noted for the courts of hustings, or the courts for proof of public claims. Either these courts continued as before, or their responsibilities were assumed by members of the Committee of Safety in the same fashion previously noted.[54]

One new court was created during this 1775 legislative session—a three judge Admiralty Court with jurisdiction over all vessels and their cargoes. The justices were to be appointed by the colonial Committee of Safety, and to the latter group— acting as the court of last resort—all appeals were to be directed. This temporary judicial system, excluding the Admiralty Court, was terminated by the adoption in 1776 of the Constitution of the Commonwealth of Virginia.[55]

CHAPTER FOUR

Virginia and the Birth of American Jurisprudence 1776–1803

Just prior to the meeting of the Continental Congress in June of 1776, and the subsequential adoption of the Declaration of Independence, the delegates from throughout Virginia met in a General Convention of Delegates and Representative at the capital in Williamsburg on May 6th for the purpose of establishing a Constitution for the Commonwealth of Virginia. First order of business was the passage of a Virginia Bill of Rights (also referred to as the Virginia Declaration of Rights)— and such a declaration was passed by the convention on June 12, 1776.[1] Included in the declaration were several fundamental rights which the Virginians were determined to have in the state constitution. The first item of which notice is taken, was not actually a right, but rather a reaction to the lack of "separation of powers" throughout their colonial history: thus they specified a government with the legislative dominant, and with both it and the executive separate from the judiciary. They declared that the people had certain inherent rights—since all powers derive from the people—to reform or abolish their government, and that the legislative and executive branches should be required to frequently account to the people by means of elections based on complete male suffrage. In reference to judiciary rights they listed the right in all criminal cases to be informed of the nature of the charge(s), to confront one's accuser and adverse witnesses, to a trial by a jury of one's peers—whose unanimous consent was required to determine a guilty verdict; and, that no one should be required to testify against himself.[2] Furthermore, that no man should suffer unusual or cruel punishments, nor excessive fines or bail, that he was not to be deprived of his liberty or property except through due process and the judgement of his peers; nor, in reference to property, to be deprived of such without the judgement of a jury. And, now a new addition to the rights demanded by the rebels of Virginia—that of religious freedom. It was decreed that all men should have the right to worship God in their own way—as their own conscience should dictate.[3]

The Constitution of Virginia was ratified by the convention on the 29th of June, 1776, and thus was placed into law the rights and desires as the people had expressed just previously in the Virginia Bill of Rights. In establishing the separation of powers principle, the delegates inserted the following provision that no individual or group shall exercise the powers of more than one branch of government at a time. But, they made one exception: the justices of the county courts were to be eligible to sit in either of the two houses of the legislature. The judiciary structure was to be modified only slightly—that is, by the addition of an appellate court of last resort. This court, to be entitled the "Supreme Court of Appeals," was to be placed into operation as of such a date as the legislature should direct.[4]

Because the connection between the original source of authority and the government of Virginia had been severed by the hate of a terribly cruel war between the mother country and her American offspring, the Virginia courts of oyer and terminer[5] (often used to describe trial courts and those of last resort) had been without legal authority to operate since the late spring of 1775.[6] Although the counties had been operating their courts since December of 1775 through the auspices of five judges appointed from the county Committees of Safety,[7] no provision had been made for the colonial Committee of Safety to assume the original jurisdiction of the inoperative General Court. Only the appellate jurisdiction had been authorized by the General Assembly in late 1775.[8] In fact, the reason for the judicial legislation in May of 1776 was the lack of any more room in the public jail in Williamsburg. This was the facility where prisoners awaiting trial in the General Court had been detained. The action of the legislative enactment is hereby recorded.

Whereas, by the dissolution of the government exercised by the King of Great Britain, courts of oyer and terminer cannot now be held for the trial of criminals committed to the public jail, it is necessary that some temporary mode should be directed for bringing them to a speedy trial.

Therefore, it is hereby enacted by the General Assembly of the Commonwealth of Virginia, that five commissioners are to be chosen by joint ballot of both houses, and that they shall meet on the 3rd Thursday in January next at the capital, in the City of Williamsburg, and there to hold a court of oyer and terminer, for the trial of said criminals in the public jail.[9]

In the October 1777 legislative session, one of the first judicial actions undertaken by the assembly was to pass a resolution declaring, that "although the distressing circumstances which formally caused us to recommend that the courts stop all law suit trials with certain exceptions, are still with us, we reverse our previous position and request that the courts proceed with any and all judiciary business in the usual manner."[10] During the second session of that year the General Assembly approved an act for establishing a court with jurisdiction in equity—the "High Court of Chancery." The said court was to consist of three judges appointed by the General Assembly, and were to hold office on their good behavior. The new court was to have jurisdiction by appeal from any inferior court, by certiorari, and through original jurisdiction, all cases with a minimum value of 10 lbs. sterling or 2,000 lbs. tobacco. Exceptions to the minimum were granted to each and every case in which the defendant was a justice of an inferior court or the vestry of a parish. The court was provided with two court session a year, in April and September; but, for the purpose of granting injunctions, writs of ne exeat, or other processes previously allowed by law, it was to be an open-door court at all times.[11]

The next judiciary related act was the re-establishment of the General Court with a new and updated definition of its powers. The most important change enacted, was the elimination of the executive branch from membership on the bench. This was the first time in the one hundred and approximately forty-year history of this court, that the bench was not comprised of the executive leaders of the government. Instead, the court was to consist of five judges, non-members of the executive and legislative branches, and who were to hold office during good behavior. The first judge nominated was to be the chief judge, with the order of appointment deciding seniority among the remainder. Any three justices were to constitute a quorum for business.[12] The court was declared to have jurisdiction over all matters, both civil and criminal, with original and appellate jurisdiction; through original suits, appeals from inferior courts, writ of habeas corpus, certiorari, error, superedeas, mandamus, and any other process so authorized.[13] All criminal cases of capital offenses, plus other felonies, were declared to be within the cognizance of the General Court. Civil cases had to exceed in value, 10 lbs. sterling or 2,000 lbs. tobacco; anything less being reserved for the jurisdiction of the county courts, the courts of hustings, and the justices of the peace. Again, as in the High Court of Chancery, the exception concerned all cases involving an inferior court judge or the vestry of a parish.[14]

When witnesses are to be summoned, the new law continued, the clerk of the General Court shall issue a summons to each witness specifying the location and date of appearance, the parties to the suit, and on whose behalf he or she was appearing.[15] As in the past, each party to a suit was to be limited to three witnesses to any one fact in contention.[16] If a witness was unable to appear, an affidavit or certificate, containing the reasons for non-appearance, signed and issued by any justice, must be delivered to the clerk of the court; whereon, the court was to award a commission for taking the deposition of said witness de bene esse, with the sworn testimony subsequently being read in open court. Prior to the taking of such a deposition, however, the party so commissioned, shall ensure that ample notice is provided to the adverse party as to time and place—so stated the law. In those cases where a party to a suit had only one witness, the General Court was not authorized to require the personal appearance if the individual requested that his testimony be taken by deposition.[17]

The new law stated that all witnesses who were required to appear in person for trials at the General Court, were to be paid at the rate of 2 lbs. tobacco or four pences per mile for their travel to and from the court. And while in attendance, the rate was to be 60 lbs. tobacco or ten shillings per day. And each witness, appearing in court, as in the past, was to be free from arrest of civil matters; and, while traveling to and from court, was to be allowed one day travel for each twenty miles.

The General Court, while conducting its judicial business, was to thoroughly and without exception inquire into, and determine, the legality of the evidence as established by the laws of the commonwealth. Upon being notified by the clerk of the General Court, the sheriff of the county was instructed to select jurors for any impending civil trial from among the bystanders, to impanel them as a jury, and to emphasize to them that they were the triers of the facts.[18] "If the General Court from this day forth, declared the legislature, upon exercising its appellate jurisdiction in a case, affirms the original verdict, the appellant shall be liable for extra damages plus the cost of ten per centum per annum upon the principal sum and costs assessed by the trial court."[19]

The 1777 legislature then laid down the following guidelines for writs of supersedeas, certiorari, and habeas corpus. Concerning the writ of supersedeas, it was enacted that any person desiring said writ had to petition the General Court with a justification of error emphasized upon which the writ was to be issued. The existence of the alleged error had to be substantiated by the opinion, stated in open court, by an attorney who regularly pleaded cases in the General Court.[20] Any party desiring to remove a case pending in any inferior court into the General Court, providing the same was cognizable under the original jurisdiction of the high court, a writ of certiorari could be granted upon good cause and ten days notice to the adverse party.[21] A writ of habeas corpus was to be utilized for the purpose of transferring a prisoner of any county jail, upon his request, to the public jail of the General Court. The clerk of the court, upon receiving such a request from a prisoner, and after determining the facts of the imprisonment and that the cause was one cognizable by the General Court, was to issue said writ for execution.[22]

In order to pressure the General Court to bring those incarcerated for treason, or other felonies, swiftly to trial—and for eventual relief of those accused if such was not accomplished—the 1777 legislature passed into law a statute of limitations. This statute stated that any such offender, who petitioned the court to be tried at the next session, and who subsequently was not so tried, was to be granted bail by a judge of the court for his appearance at the court session following. And then, if by the end of that second court session, the prisoner was still without indictment or trial, he was to be released immediately without any fear that he might in the future be subject to arrest upon the same charges.[23]

Although the examining courts had been in existence for almost one hundred and forty years as an unofficial county level court, it was not formally recognized by law until October of 1777. The first part of the law stated that any person, except a slave, who was charged with a crime before a justice of the peace, which in his judgement constituted an offence within the jurisdiction of the county court, or the General Court, he was thereby required to take recognizance of all witnesses to appear before said court and commit the offender to the county jail. The justice would then have the county sheriff notify the other justices of the peace to meet jointly within five to ten days for the purpose of holding an examining court. If the decision of that court was to hold the prisoner for the county court, he was to be released on bail pending the next session of the grand jury. However, if the decision was to forward his case to the General Court, the justices were required to take the depositions of all witnesses and have sworn those whose testimony they deemed to be material, relevant, and competent, to appear when summoned by the court. Then the offender was to be transferred to the public jail in Williamsburg; again, bail being arranged if the individual could afford it.[24]

Upon receipt of notice of a case being thus referred, the clerk of the county from thence the case was being removed, issued a writ of venire facias to the sheriff. This writ required that twelve jurors were to be selected from those residents of the crime scene vicinity to meet as a jury on the sixth day of next session of the General Court. Those of the twelve who were not challenged, plus substitutes from among the bystanders, would comprise a lawful jury. The said jurors, to be reimbursed in the same manner as witnesses, were to be paid out of the public funds.[25] In the majority of cases, a trial jury of this period was only held responsible as trier of the facts; but, this division of fact from law was one of jury discretion. If a jury believed that the trial judge in any particular case was unduly biased, they could undertake to decide both the law and the facts.[26]

The legislative arm of the government further decided that defendants who desired certain witnesses to be summoned on his behalf, whether at an examining or county court, or at the General Court, were entitled to have a subpoena issued accordingly. Travel and attendance fees were to continue to be paid in the same manner as for witnesses in civil cases; that is, at the same rate, and out of the prisoner's own pockets. In addition, subject to possible conviction, should the defendant have sufficient estate to cover the costs of prosecution, the courts were to be required to so order.

All General Court grand juries were ordered to have twenty-four freeholders. These men were to be selected and summoned by the sheriff of the county wherein the court was to be held (to be decided according to the geographical origin of the majority of cases), to appear at the next session of the court. They were to be charged with inquiring into, and making presentment of all cases involving treason, murder, and other crimes of a felonious nature. Upon notice of a capital offense, and provided that the court docket allowed, the General Court was ordered to arraign the prisoner at once; with trial to be held at the earliest possible date before a petit jury of his peers.[27]

During the spring session of the following year, 1778, the legislature increased the sessions of the General Court to four per year—the extra two sessions to be devoted to criminal cases only. This measure was to ensure a shorter period of confinement, or liability to bail restrictions, and initiate swifter justice for all parties.[28] That fall, during the second annual session of the legislature, a modification to the length of time a capital offense prisoner could be held without indictment and trial was enacted. It was decided that following the second session of the General Court the prisoner would not be acquitted, if, the prosecution could show good cause as to why a request for trial had hot been forth coming. However, if a third session passed with no trial, the prisoner was to be acquitted of all charges and immediately released.[29]

The major judicial enactment of the fall session of 1778 was the creation of the "Supreme Court of Appeals," as dictated by the Virginia Constitution of 1776. This was the first time in the history of Virginia's judicial system, that the court of last resort was not also an arm of the executive or legislative bodies. Appeals to this court were to come from the inferior courts, both by way of the General Court, The High Court of Chancery, and the Admiralty Court. The bench of this court of last resort was to consist of three teams of judges: the judges of the General Court and three assistant judges, appointed by the General Assembly, if the case in question came from The High Court of Chancery; or, the three assistant judges and the judges of The High Court of Chancery, when the case had its origin in the General Court. Whenever a case originated in the Court of Admiralty, or in special cases of state interest from one of the aforementioned inferior courts, all of the previously noted judges would constitute the bench of the Court of Appeals. In such cases, the justices of The High Court of Chancery would be the senior judges.[30] The court, which was to hold two six-day sessions a year—in March and August—was given jurisdiction over all cases which originated on an appeal or petition from The High Court of Chancery or the Court of Admiralty, or, by writs of error from the General Court, and also from other inferior courts under special circumstances. Whenever the appeal judges found themselves evenly divided on an issue, declared the legislature, the decision of the last inferior court was to stand as final.[31]

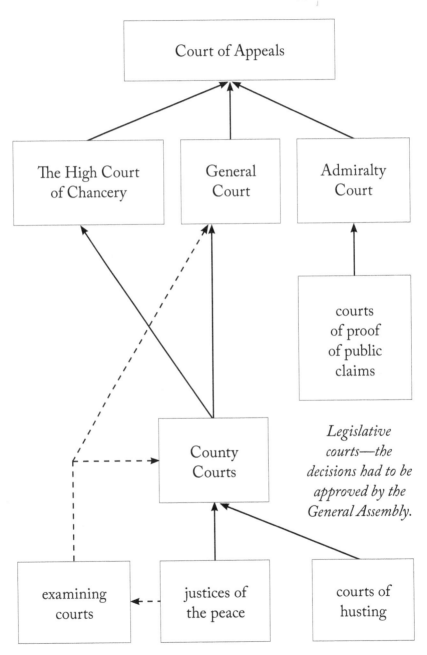

FIGURE 15: COURT SYSTEM OF THE
COMMONWEALTH OF VIRGINIA, 1778

In November of 1777 the thirteen colonies, in joint convention, adopted the Articles of Confederation and Perpetual Union as the governing compact of all the colonies in one body politic. Final ratification came in March of 1781.[32] In reference to jurisprudence the articles stated that the congress of the government was to be the final judge of all disputes between two or more states. Upon congress receiving a petition from a state in dispute with another—said petition stating the nature of the controversy—it was to notify the other party and assign a day for an appointed official of each state to appear before it in session. These state officials, by joint agreement would be instructed to select judges to constitute a court for hearing of the differences between them; but, if this body of judges was unable to arrive at a determination of the issue, congress would then be required to select three individuals from each state. By process of challenge by the disputing parties, the list would be reduced to thirteen names, and then, congress would select by lot no less than seven, nor more than nine men, to form a court. Of those selected, four were to constitute a quorum, and a majority vote would be deemed sufficient to tender a legal decision. This decision was to be final. Since the possibility existed that the court could divide evenly, and with the articles failing to specify the subsequent procedure in such an event, it appears that congress could either initial the same procedure over, or itself act as the court of last resort.[33]

By 1787, however, it was clear to all astute and observing persons that the Articles of Confederation worked poorly and only with great difficulty—and the national judiciary was nothing more than a poor joke. Meeting in Philadelphia, Pennsylvania, in late May of 1787, the delegates from the various states, who publicly at least, were only supposed to revise the articles, had by September created a constitution based on the principle of federalism with three separate branches to constitute the new national government: the legislative, the executive, and the judiciary.[34]

The federal judiciary of the United States was established under Articles III of the new constitution. Only one court was established by this constitution, the Supreme Court of the United States. Section one reads as follows:

> The judicial power of the United States shall be vested in one Supreme Court, and in such inferior courts as the Congress may from time to time ordain and establish. The judges, both of the Supreme Court and inferior courts, should hold their offices during good behavior, and shall, at stated times, receive for their services, a compensation, which shall not be diminished during their continuance in office.[35]

Section two, part one, describes the extent and limits of the jurisdiction of the Supreme Court and the other federal courts to be established. Part two of that section was enacted for the purpose of detailing the area of original jurisdiction—which is limited in scope, and the all-inclusive appellate jurisdiction. Part three of section two notes the right to a trial by jury, except in cases of impeachment. And the last section, number three, deals with the definition of treason. Federal judges, declared the new constitution, were to be appointed by the President with the consent of the Senate—the upper house of the legislative body.[36]

Holding the federalist politicians to their promise, Madison, on June 8, 1789, introduced a number of proposed constitutional amendments to the House of Representatives—amendments that were designed to safeguard the rights of every citizen. Referred to as the Bill of Rights, the twelve amendments, reduced to ten, were passed by Congress on September 25, 1789, and ratified by three-fourths of the states by December 15, 1791.[37] Those amendment with relevancy to the courts and judicial process were the 1st, 4th, 5th, 6th, 7th, and 8th. The first amendment prohibits any establishment of a state church, guarantees freedoms of worship, press, peaceable assembly, and petition; the fourth protects the citizens against unreasonable searches and seizures by governmental authorities, except on "probable cause"; and, the fifth guarantees that no one shall be held liable to answer for any capital offenses except on indictment by a grand jury (except in the military), to be placed in double jeopardy, to be a witness against one's self, nor to be deprived of life, liberty, or property, except by due process of law. The sixth amendment set the requirement that every accused should have the right to a speedy and public trial by jury, to know the charges, to confront his accuser and all adverse witnesses, and to have the assistance of counsel; the seventh, pertaining to civil disputes, created the right to a jury wherever the value was more than twenty dollars; and, the eighth amendment specified that excessive bail and fines were prohibited.[38]

During the interval between the end of the Constitutional Convention in September of 1787 and ratification by the last state to do so, Rhode Island, on May 29, 1790, controversy raged within and out of the various state legislatures. In Virginia, in June of 1788, during the height of the debates, George Mason spoke out against the proposed constitution in the Virginia Assembly by stressing the fear that a government under its alleged guidance would be inclined to become dictatorial. Rising in answer to Mr. Mason was a constitutional advocate, destined to become the father of American jurisprudence, Mr. John Marshall. Contained within the answer of this thirty-two-year-old man was a prophecy relevant to the future cornerstone of the American system of jurisprudence.

With respect to its cognizance in all cases arising under the Constitution and the laws of the United States, he says that the laws of the United States being paramount to the laws of the particular states, there is no case but what will extend to. Has the government of the United

States power to make laws on every subject? Can they go beyond the delegated powers? If they were to make a law not warranted by any of the powers enumerated, it would be considered by the judges as an infringement of the constitution which they are to guard. They would not consider such a law as coming under their jurisdiction. They would declare it void.

Mr. Marshall went on to quote Mr. Mason: "How disgraceful is it that the state courts cannot be trusted!" Marshall replied that the federal constitution would not take away their jurisdiction, that it was necessary that the national courts should have jurisdiction over those cases which were bound to occur under the constitution and the federal laws. Whose courts could possibly have cognizance except the federal courts, Marshall asked. The purpose of such courts, he stressed, would be to prevent violence, to stop bloodshed before it started; and therefore, what other court system could be as important.[40]

Another advocate of America's constitutional birth, who probably did more than anyone else to ensure its eventual success, also foresaw the concept of constitutional review as the foundation of American judiciary. Alexander Hamilton, the most prolific of the authors of the Federalist papers—written as part of the campaign to ensure ratification of the constitution—implied that the idea of the proposed federal judiciary having the power to declare acts of congress as being in violation of the constitution, and therefore null and void, as being a common item of the controversy surrounding the new proposed government. In the seventy-eighth article of the Federalist Papers, Hamilton stated his views of such national judicial powers in the following fashion.

There is no position which depends on clearer principles than that every act of a delegated authority, contrary to the tenor of the commission under which it is exercised, is void. No legislative act, therefore, contrary to the Constitution, can be valid. To deny this would be to affirm that the deputy is greater than his principal; that the servant is above his master; that the representatives of the people are superior to the people themselves; that men acting by virtue of powers may do not only what their powers do not authorize, but what they forbid.

The interpretation of the laws is the proper and peculiar province of the courts. A constitution is, in fact, and must be regarded by the judges as, a fundamental law. It therefore belongs to them to ascertain its meaning as well as the meaning of any particular act proceeding from the legislative body. If there should happens to be an irreconcilable variance between the two, that which has the superior obligation and validity ought, of course, to be preferred; or, in other words, the Constitution ought to be preferred to the statute, the intention of the people to the intention of their agents.[41]

By the spring of 1789, the new Constitution of the United States of America was manifested in the blood, frame, and sinew of an operating government, with its separate branches off to a creaking, stumbling start—but, nevertheless, working! During this first session of the new federal congress only one other legislative bill equaled the Bill of Rights in its impact on the healthy growth, vitality, and historical longevity of the national constitution: The Judiciary Act of 1789.[42] Enacted into law on September 24, 1789, this act established for the federal judiciary what the constitution itself had only suggested: the membership of the Supreme Court, the establishment of inferior courts, the jurisdiction of each type of court, and other details necessary to breathe life into the national court system.

The first section stated that the Supreme Court was to consist of a chief justice and five associate justices, any four of whom were to constitute a quorum. The court was to hold two sessions annually. Sections two and three established the district Courts, one for each state with a single judge sitting. These courts were to have four sessions annually. Furthermore, that said districts—excepting Maine and Kentucky—were to be divided into three circuits known as the eastern, middle, and southern circuits, and that in each district, annually, a circuit court would sit twice a year. The Circuit Courts would consist of two Supreme Court justices and a district court judge from that circuit. However, the act specified that no district court judge could sit on an appeal or writ of error from his own trial decision.[43]

The district courts were given cognizance of all matters arising under federal laws in the states constituting their district: original jurisdiction of all admiralty and maritime cases; concurrent jurisdiction with the states or circuit courts of all causes involving an alien suing for tort only in violation of international law or a treaty of the United States; jurisdiction in all cases, concurrent with the circuits courts, where the United States was suing in a matter valued higher than one hundred dollars; and, exclusive jurisdiction over all suits against consuls or vice-consuls, with the exception previously mentioned. And in the district courts, with the exception of admiralty and maritime matters, jury trial was declared to be mandatory. The circuit courts were declared to have original jurisdiction, concurrent with the states, of all civil suits at common law or in equity valued higher than five hundred dollars, and where the United States was a party: or citizens of different states are the opposing adversaries; and, of course, appellate jurisdiction over cases coming from the district courts.[44]

Reference to the jurisdiction of the Supreme Court was done through the authority under section thirteen to issue writs of prohibition to the district courts in matters of admiralty and maritime; and, writs of mandamus where warranted to inferior courts and all persons holding office in the government of the United States.[45]

In early March of 1801, just before Thomas Jefferson assumed the office of President of the United States, John Adams, the outgoing President signed a commission for one William Marbury, appointing him to the judicial office of a justice of the peace for the District of Columbia. Then the seal of the United States was affixed to it, and the Secretary of State, John Marshall, ordered the commission delivered. However, the new Secretary of State, James Madison, found the commission undelivered on the office desk. The new administration refused to deliver the commission, and Marbury filed suit against the Secretary of State. The Chief Justice of the United States, as of March 1801, immediately after Jefferson became President, was John Marshall. Although nominated in February 1801, and confirmed by the Senate prior to new administration assuming office, Marshall was not sworn in until after March 4th. In response to Marbury's suit Madison was ordered to show cause why a writ of mandamus should not be issued, directing him to deliver the commission.[46]

The case reached the Supreme Court in 1803, where Chief Justice Marshall and the Associate Justices heard and determined the case. The questions involved were as follows:

1. Has the applicant a right to the commission he demands?
2. If that right has been violated, do the laws of the United States afford him a remedy?
3. Is this remedy a mandamus issuing from this Supreme Court?[47]

The court decided yes to the first two questions, and no to the third question. The reason that a writ of mandamus could not be issued by the Supreme Court in the opinion delivered by Chief Justice Marshall, was that this would have been an exercise of original jurisdiction not authorized by the Constitution. The Constitution defined the areas of original jurisdiction as applicable to the Supreme Court, and the matter in dispute was not included therein. The Chief Justice concluded the opinion, which repudiated that section of the 1789 Judiciary Act previously referred to as section thirteen, by impregnating into the American judicial philosophy that concept which he had suggested to the Virginia constitutional ratifying convention fifteen years before that of constitutional review.

The particular phraseology of the Constitution of the United States confirms and strengthens the principle, supposed to be essential to all written constitutions, that a repugnant to the constitution is void, and that courts, as well as other departments, are bound by that instruments.[48]

CHAPTER FIVE

American Jurisprudence: Opinions and Analysis of Its Roots

I n any discussion of American judicial heritage, the subject of "common law," what it is, and the fact that its roots are buried in the remote shadows of English antiquity, is a topic that is impossible to ignore if a complete understanding of our system of justice is to be gained. And although such a discussion is not indispensable in order to understand either the basic substance of, nor the molding influence of the various forces which shaped and impregnated American jurisprudence during its infant years of colonial development, such an omission would constitute a philosophical void that would forever remain a haunting suggestion of unfulfilled knowledge.

To assist us in undertaking the aforementioned task, we shall first of all, turn to three American lawyers who practiced law during the early years of the 19th century, and whose nearness to the colonial period allowed them to view the influence of the common law on our colonial history with a clarity that neither the occupants of the twentieth century, nor those who lived in the colonial period could possibly achieve. But yet, we are not to expect complete agreement even among these front row spectators of our developing system of jurisprudence. Let us begin.

The first witness to be called to present his testimony is one Peter S. DuPonceau, who delivered an address to the students of the Law Academy of Philadelphia in the year 1824.[1] In his testimony he pointed out that the force behind our system of jurisprudence—our civil institutions—is that unseen but ever present force called the "common law." This common law has been shaped by the forces of circumstances to an American mold, and given an imminence as the foundation of our federal constitution. It is, Mr. DuPonceau claimed, a force that is felt by every citizen: through federal laws, state laws, county and municipal ordinances, and the customs and mores of the people.[2] The grievances which caused the colonists to tear themselves apart from Great Britain were violations of this common law; but, when completed—in fact, while the separating was taking place—they claimed adherence and loyalty to the common law. This was because they considered the common law and the British Constitution to be one and the same; and since their rebellion had commenced on the belief that their rights as British subjects had been violated, they saw themselves as the defenders, and the mother county as the violator of the common law.[3]

The separation, however, and the subsequent establishment of a written constitution created a major difference between America's relationship to the common law as opposed to that of Great Britain. In the mother country, Mr. DuPonceau declared, it is still the energy source for their system of jurisprudence; while in our country, although we still cherish it for the development of freedoms through the ages, and the direct benefits which it had bestowed on us, it is no longer the source of judicial power, but rather the means of implementation. However, this was not a change that came about overnight. The idea of the

English common law remaining the source of our system of jurisprudence continued to persist during the initial years of our federal republic; the constitution being viewed as the funnel through which the English common law had to pass in order to be applicable to American conditions.[4]

However, the new federal judiciary early on had the opportunity to create a distinct and unique American relationship to the common law, and without hesitation, proceeded to execute that difference. Various criminal cases entered into the cognizance of the federal courts over which jurisdiction from both the constitution and federal laws appeared to be lacking—but, with the belief that the common law provided the needed jurisdiction. Fear mounted among some elements of the American public, that, if the federal judiciary adopted that line of reasoning their power would be unlimited. The federal courts, however, quickly laid such fears to rest with the precedent shaping decisions which established the constitution of the United States as the source and limiting authority of all governmental powers, executive and legislative, as well as judicial.[5]

Taking a position which can only be described as an extreme anti-common law position—entirely at odds with the respectful awe of our first witness—are the views of Mr. John Milton Goodenow, attorney-at-law, of the State of Ohio. Author of a book contrasting the principles of American jurisprudence with English common law, we shall first look at the exact manner in which this witness presents his testimony, lest we lose our sense of perspective. His opening statement is shocking and radical.

> The common law of England had its origin, and received its impression and perfection even down to the time when our ancestors left England, in dark, uncultivated and barbarous ages; suited to an ignorant and blood-thirsty people; under the tutelage of turbulent,

haughty, sacrilegious tyrants and dictators; that as a code, separate from Statue law, it is without beauty, symmetry, or even shape; undefinable and immeasurable; bloody in its maxims; inhuman in its policies; and entirely diverse and repugnant to the philosophy and christian refinement of this country.[6]

Mr. Goodenow continued from his initial onslaught with the observation that the government of Great Britain, in his day, had yet to enjoy the principles of freedoms and rights secured by the American colonists through their revolution against the British Crown.[7] Even in the year of 1819 the British criminal code showed less concern for human life and rights, he alleged, than their civil code did for the rights of property. In the time of King Alfred many crimes were punished by monetary fines which were paid in part to the families of the victims; but in the reign of King George III, it was claimed there were 160 capital offenses, plus 500 other penal offenses in the Criminal Code of England.[8] An accused in the mother country, in 1819, was alleged to frequently be devoid of counsel, denied the right to call witnesses on his own behalf; while at the same time it was being declared that a speedy trial was somehow a benefit to the people. The king and his ministers, cried our witness, do not hesitate where their interest is served, to strike down the due process of law, arbitrarily confine offenders so that they cannot easily be subject to a writ of habeas corpus. In reference to speedy trials in the England of his day, our witness placed himself on record.

> A speedy trial—precipitancy in depriving a man of his life is certainly one of the most palpable marks of the inhumanity and injustice of human laws.[9]

The American government, it was claimed, was endowed with a superiority, with a stability, which was derived from a set of powers which were unchangeable except by a legally prescribed and publically controlled method of alteration. This was held to be the essence of the security of freedom, seen in the legislative halls, observed and experienced in the judicial proceedings of a free people. On the other side of the Atlantic, however, our witness indicates with a sneer, we are told of the awe in which the early 19th century English held the political theories of freedom; but, that the incestuous political struggles, and the suffering of the people, revealed a social instability and decay that will long endue.[10] The British Parliament was credited with no standard against which to judge their principles. The common law is whatever they say it is—and consequently, "…has a doctrine to suit every age and every purpose, but that of freedom. Liberty has there no resting place."[11]

If a safe, secure, and happy society is to be the only reference guide for human punishment, Goodenow claimed, then the answer has to be that the criminal law of a state is separate from the government, that its foundations are secured and authorized by the necessity of our society to engage in self-preservation.

> The judge, therefore, of a criminal tribunal, is governed himself by positive, and executes and enforces the will of the supreme power, which is the will of the people, in their aggregate capacity and not the private right or private will of an individual.[12]

It was thus subsequently derived that the severity of criminal justice should be in direct proportion to the need which self-preservation imposes on the community; and that justice, modified by the social refinements and customs, can only be dispersed equally when regulated by a supreme power. This power, if freedom is to be preserved, can only evolve from a supreme law—a written constitution.[13]

Another favorable advocate of our common law heritage was Judge Zephaniah Swift, who in 1810, was a judge of the Supreme Court of the State of Connecticut. His opening statement was as favorable to the concept of the common law as that of Mr. Goodenow was negative.

> The superiority of the common law, to any other code extant, may in a great measure, be attributed to two fortunate circumstances, originally peculiar to that country in which it originated; these are, trial by jury; and the publication of Reports of the Adjudications of their courts by assigning to the jury the province of deciding questions of fact, and to the court questions of law; a distinction has always been kept up between law and fact, highly favorable to the decisions of points of law, and which could hardly have been obtained where they are blended together. When both are decided by the court—the two must be kept apart.[14]

The courts, wrote Judge Swift, have an inherent discretion of modifying their rules according to the peculiarities of each case that come under their cognizance. This a vital principle of our judiciary, both state and federal, correcting decisions of the past to meet the needs of the present, borrowing when required from other countries, deciding and molding law in areas that the legislature has yet to enter in.[15]

In reference to the interpretation of the English courts of his time, Judge Swift declared, that to the extent that they are logical deductions from the common law, shared by both countries, they are to be respected; and by the same rule, the extent to which they depart there from, they are to be ignored. However, the time is coming when American common law will have developed a depth, which of itself, will be sufficient to guide the American judiciary through all future uncharted waters of potential judicial interpretation.[16] In the opinion of this early 19th century judge, there is no area of law more important than that of the law of evidence. It is only now, he stressed, in the early years of our republic, that such rules have been reduced to a point of refinement that actually aides the preservation our continuous search for truth and justice.[17]

Following just a few years after the judicial observations of the witnesses presented to this point, one of foreign birth and citizenship had the occasion to tour the young American nation and record his observations. This young gentleman, Alexis de Tocqueville, a man of aristocratic birth and position, and consequently whose very background enhanced the credibility of his generally positive commentary on American life, government, and customs, recorded one of the most complete and objective analysis of American jurisprudence that has ever been executed.

Tocqueville commenced his commentary by noting that there are basic characteristics of judicial powers in all nations: the duty of arbitration; pronouncement on special cases, rather than general principles—although in so doing, such principles are subject to modification or nullification; and, its inability to initial judicial action of its own accord. The American judiciary, he noted, has all these characteristics—but nevertheless, are endowed with a unique and precedence-setting power. The citizenry of the American nation, he observed, have acquiesced in the right of their judges to base their decisions on the American Constitution rather than statute law—that is, to render null and void those laws which they interpret to be at variance with the constitution. It was, he noted, referred to as "judicial review."[18]

Tocqueville was amazed that all elements of the American public supported this unique judicial characteristic—that he was unable to find anyone who thought otherwise, even when they disagreed with a particular decision. In England, he pointed out, the constitution is nothing more than the unwritten common law, and therefore parliament is at once a constitutional and legislative assembly. Thus their constitution is in a state of perpetual change. The American constitution was observed as standing between the British model, just mentioned, and that of France which was immutable to change. It is just as binding on the congress as on the individual, because it is the will of the people; and, although not to be trifled with lightly, it can be changed by a formally prescribed set of rules.[19]

The distinguished Frenchman observed that in England it would be unthinkable to grant their judiciary the power of overruling the legislative body; which also, constituted the court of last resort, and, from whose membership were selected the executive leadership. Consequently, no law passed by parliament could conceivably be unconstitutional.[20]

The American idea of constitutional review, and the manner in which it is accomplished, Tocqueville concluded, are truly unique in the history of jurisprudence. By linking the nullification of laws with the interest of private citizens, and only to those laws brought before the court by cases in dispute, the prosecution of the law with that of an individual, the legislature is rebuked—but, without a direct and public attack—and free of political abuse while the ultimate end is being observed: the freedom of the people. Consequently, said Tocqueville:

> Within these limits, the power vested in American courts of justice of pronouncing a statute to be unconstitutional, forms one of the most powerful barriers which has ever been devised against the tyranny of political assemblies.[21]

Our French witness then observed that in both the United States and her mother county the view is held that tyranny and political oppression are to be treated like other crimes by diluting the penalty and making for greater ease of conviction. In both countries, he continued, the initial step in coping with political crimes is through political jurisdiction—wherein one house of the legislature impeaches and the other acts as the trial court. Then, however, the difference in method is revealed. The English Parliament is empowered to inflict all the dispositions of the penal code, and thus there is hesitation to use it—until it may be too late. In the United States, however, he noted that the congress is limited to stripping the offender of his public office and leaves any further proceedings to the judiciary. The Americans have established an administrative action of public discipline which is clothed with the formalities of a judicial decision. The judicial system of the United States, Tocqueville concluded, is much more flexible and harmonious in its relationship to the remainder of the governmental machinery—and with less severe political consequences than that system found in Great Britain.[22]

The American system of jurisprudence as described by our four witnesses: Peter DuPonceau, John Goodenow, Zephaniah Swift, and Alexis de Tocqueville, possesses great similarities to that of Great Britain; but is, at the same time, distinctly American. What were the forces which gave it being, which shaped and molded it into its unique version of the Advocacy/Accusatorial System? The answer has to start with the two most important developments in the history of the western world since the birth of the Christian Religion: the Protestant Reformation, which established a major precedence in man's ageless struggle to free his mind from the slavery of ignorance; and, the launching of the Age of Discovery, which was the vehicle that carried the continuation of that struggle to the freer environment of the New World—the American wilderness.[23]

The Reformation, initiated by Martin Luther, was subsequently duplicated by John Calvin, plus others—and the shock waves were felt again and again like an endless tsunami sweeping outward from an earthquake on the ocean floor. England of the 16th and 17th centuries was torn asunder by the social, political, and economic upheavals caused by this schism within Christianity. Specifically, England in this period was experiencing the religious and social disarray of a Puritan revolution centered in the midst of an economic transition from the old feudalistic society into a society based on capitalism.[24]

On the surface, the Puritan revolt was against the Church of England: it ranged from those who merely wanted to reform the church, to correct some deviances, to those who had concluded that reform was impossible, and consequently, that separation was the only path. Although a religious struggle, it was also a rebellion of the middle class whose mercantile interests demanded a larger measure of freedom than the king and his landed aristocracy were about to allow. The struggle was part of the beginning of the road to capitalistic economies and parliamentary governments. It is only against this background that we can hope to understand the development of our republican form of government, and subsequently, the vast array of rights and protections which each American citizen is entitled to have under our system of jurisprudence.

The three religious groups that emerged from the English social, economic, and religious turmoil by the beginning of the 17th century were the Anglicans, the Presbyterians, and the Independents. The first group adhered to the absolutism of church and state, the second were for a more liberal society—a compromise between aristocratic and democratic principles by a desired substitution of a selected aristocracy for that of heritage—and the third party, which was democratic in thought and purpose. Among the latter, those who were referred to as Separatists constituted the extreme left-wing element of the Puritan movement. They inclined to a concept of individualism that became in practice the conception of Christian democracy. They believed that a true church was a congregation of brothers. Standing to the left of the Separatists, but as an individual, not as a group, was the Seeker—an open-minded questioner of the nature of the true church. Such a man was Roger Williams, expelled from the Massachusetts Bay Colony during its first decade in the New World. The teachings of Luther, inclining to tolerance of differences of opinion, formed the religious foundation of the Seekers and Separatists; while Calvinism was a foe of differences of religious opinion, and of equalitarianism. It saw little good in human nature and enacted very strict rules of behavior.

The immigrants who settled in Massachusetts Bay and Virginia were Puritan Presbyterians who believed that they represented the true nature of the Anglican church, but who were opposed to the church's leadership, whom they believed to be in error. The Massachusetts Bay Puritans and the Separatists, also known as the Pilgrims, had little in common socially. The leaders of Massachusetts Bay were basically country gentlemen— halfway between the aristocracy and the merchant class, while the entire Separatist colony of New Plymouth was of plebeian origins.[26] The first settlers in Virginia were also Puritans, but unlike their northern brethren, they had not come to the New World for religious reasons, but for economic opportunity. Their membership, although spread over the entire spectrum of social classes, was for the most part comprised of small-town folks.[27]

The Separatists of New Plymouth Colony brought two basic principles to New England: the democratic church, and the principles of a democratic state. When John Winthrop and the other leaders of Massachusetts Bay arrived ten years later, they were faced with the problem of erecting a social order. They were forced by the wilderness,[28] like the Virginia settlers before them, to discard their adherence to the idea of centralized control of church—not realizing that such control was absolutely essential to the long-term survival of Calvinism. Since the wilderness gave them no choice, they logically adopted the New Plymouth concept of Congregationalism; each community parish being independent of the others—thus circumventing the dangerous distances which made centralized control of church an impossibility.[29] The leadership of both Virginia and Massachusetts Bay were forced by the immense wilderness and the resulting necessity for unity,[30] to acquiesce in an ever increasing demand for governmental participation: thus democratic assemblies were introduced. By property restrictions, and required church membership, the leaders of both colonies attempted to restrict participation to the upper section of the plebeian class—in essence a yeomanry class of small property holders, in social terms, an aristocracy of selected members.[31]

In Virginia, the restoration of the English monarchy in 1660, brought Governor Berkeley back into the governor's chair. Opposed to the capitalistic tendencies of the Puritan settlers, and the independent spirit they had developed, he was desirous of transplanting a dying feudalism from England to the New world. Eventually, through his Council of State (his cabinet) and his role as a royal type governor, he was able to obtain sufficient enough ascendency over the colonial assembly to accomplish his goal. The result of his success: the establishment of what later came to be known as the plantation south.[32]

Although it was the proposed intentions of the colonial governments to adhere as closely as possible to both English statutes and the common law, there was not always a corresponding subject to which a law might be applicable; or, as in the case of nonconformity to the principles of worship in the Church of England, the very idea of enforcement was blasphemous. Furthermore, in some other colonies, like Rhode Island, Maryland, and Pennsylvania, even religious differences were tolerated. Added to the practical problem of imitating English law, there was the problem of the natural prejudices on the part of all who had fled persecution to interpret the worst from any erection of similar laws in the colonies. Then, there was the fact of differing concepts of what constituted English common law. The concept of its nature in 1607 had certainly changed by the year 1630; and, if the idea of continuous change in the common law is applicable to each colony's beginning—a period of one hundred and fifty-two years from the first settlement in Virginia to the last in Georgia—a multitude of different concepts of the common law must have existed up and down the Atlantic seaboard at any one time. Consequently, in any one colony, those aspects of the English common law which had developed after the beginning of colonial settlement, would have had no, or very little, applicability to the subsequent development of local concepts of jurisprudence. The fourth main factor which adversely effected the effort to adhere to English law, was found in the power utilized by the various colonial legislatures as influenced by the views, principles, and local circumstances of their respective populations.[33]

Backstepping for just a moment, the settlers of Massachusetts Bay carried their non-adherence to the rules of worship of the Church of England to the point of prosecuting the dissenters within their own ranks. By such a development, through the wilderness door of freedom, the colony of Rhode Island was created with its religious and politically inclined concepts of freedom.[34] Subsequently, this unique concept of limiting colonial authorities through the enactment of laws and established rights, spread gradually throughout the colonies, and eventually into the concept of written constitutions.[35]

The leaders of the early settlers of Virginia and Massachusetts did not believe in either religious freedom or political democracy. These ideas came in the minds of followers far more radical; who believed that the only true church was voluntary association of like-minded believers. This was a revolutionary concept in an age of state churches to which all were required to belong.[36] Transferred to the civil realm, the concept was truly staggering! And this was exactly the step the settlers of New Plymouth took through the enactment of the Mayflower Compact. Roger Williams carried the idea of the compact to its logical conclusion, when he declared, "The foundation of civil power lies in the people," and "A people may erect and establish what form of government seems to them most meet for their civil condition." In the 17th century the implementation of such radical ideas was possible only in places remote and difficult to reach from the intolerance of established authority in the Old World.[37]

Education played an important part in the long developing process that led to our American system of jurisprudence. Many of the formal and informal leaders of the early settlers were products of English universities. From the moment the Protestant Reformation begun, the right of private judgement was never again to be completely subservient; and, inevitably, this could have no other long range results than diversity of faith. Thus, diversity in the religious realm ultimately influenced civil, social, and governmental concepts, and subsequently, the whole system of jurisprudence. Although the early colonial leaders, as previously mentioned, were not adherents to the concept of democracy, many of them were strong supporters of education, and subsequently, schools and universities were quickly established. Consequently, these foes of democratic concepts unwittingly nourished and supported one of the many forces that was to be their undoing.[38]

One colonial leader who was not blind to the influence of education, however, was Governor Berkeley of Virginia. Around the early 1670s he answered an inquiry from the authorities of the Colony of Maryland, and in reference to education within Virginia, he had the following words to say.

I thank God, there are no free schools, nor printing, and I hope we shall not have these hundred years; for learning has brought disobedience, and heresy, and sects into the world, and printing has divulged them, and libels against the best government. God keep us from both.[39]

The forces that set in motion the germination of the seeds of American jurisprudence, that nourished, shaped, and molded them into a joint identification as one basis system can be summarized as the Protestant Reformation, the Age of Discovery which transported the released forces of the Reformation to the New World, the interaction of religious beliefs and forced utilization of democratic principles, various interpretations of the English common law up and down the Atlantic seaboard, a blind faith in education, and the remoteness from the oppressive shackles of the authorities of the Old World. But, the dominant link is still missing, that cohesive and binding force that not only projected its own influence, but which opened the flood gates for all the others: the environmental stage of the primeval wilderness. To enlighten us on this concluding note, I present the former Frederick Jackson Turner—in his time, the most distinguished of American historians.[40]

It was his belief that the frontier in American history divided the civilized from the primitive, the natural from the institutional, and the savage from the cultured. Where they met, a profound change was worked upon both. Inevitably and eventually, however, the former retreated before the latter. At the beginning, though, along the entire Atlantic seaboard, each individual colony was first altered and molded by the wilderness as their test of survival. This process was labeled by Turner as the Americanization of the settlers. The frontier was a process in which men first confronted and then mastered their savage environment. From the hunters and fur traders to the farmers of the more settled areas along the coast, each economic group had its own frontier to master. Consequently, there was a continuous series of perennial rebirths, an ongoing challenge. This continuous conflict promoted the qualities of individualism, and thus was a tremendous influence on the development of democratic concepts.[41]

Turner saw the frontier as a safety valve for all the malcontents who felt trapped by social and religious customs, or economic hardship. In the wilderness the bonds of convention were broken, and democratic equality, sooner or later, became the prevailing principle of the developing societies.[42] The tendency is anti-social, an antipathy to social control, and specifically to direct authority. This effect of the wilderness helps to explain the difficulties Virginia and Massachusetts had in maintaining non-democratic governments and strict religious control. The influence of the wilderness on the development of individualism and its group equivalency, democracy, also influenced the development of individual selfishness and a lack of tolerance of governmental actions beyond reasonable grounds. Thus there developed a laxity in in regard to governmental affairs which was a large factor in igniting the American Revolution.[43]

In conclusion, it can be seen clearly that the roots of American jurisprudence are at one and the same time, those elements which were derived from the antiquity of the Anglo-Saxon/ Norman period—constituting our English heritage—and those forces which drove our ancestors across a dangerous ocean, and helped to mold, shape, and polish one system of jurisprudence until it became another. Thus, it has been demonstrated, that the environmental influence of the primeval wilderness was an impregnating and intimidating cohesiveness, that not only projected a dominating aura over a multitude of interacting forces, to which all the American colonists were subjected—but, that by its destructive relationship with the cultural shackles of the human mind, it released the full force of individualism to impact upon the embryonic heritage of English jurisprudence— consequently—molding it into a uniquely American system.[44]

ENDNOTES

CHAPTER ONE

1. George W. Greenaway, ed., (David C. Douglas, General Editor), "Concerning Ownership: Trial by Battle, and the Grand Assize," *English Historical Documents*, Vol. II (15 Vols.; London, Eyre & Spottiswoode, 1968), 465.

2. Merlin Lewis, Warren Bundy, and James L. Hague, *An Introduction to the Courts and Judicial Process* (Englewood Cliffs: Prentice-Hall Inc., 1978), 4, 240–41, 258.

3. Henry J. Abraham, *The Judicial Process: An Introductory Analysis of the Courts of the United States, England, and France* (London: Oxford University Press, 1975), 98–99.

4. Greenaway, ed., "Concerning Ownership: Trial by Battle, and the Grand Assize," *English Historical Documents*, Vol. II, 465.

5. Lewis, Bundy, and Hague, *An Introduction to the Courts and Judicial Process*, 4, 240–41, 258.

6. Ibid., 14.

7. Ibid., 4.

8. Abraham, *The Judicial Process*, 98–100.

9. Ibid., 102.

10. Ibid., 107.

11. Ibid., 102.

12. Ibid., 110–15.

13. Ibid.

14. Ibid., 138.
15. Lewis, Bundy, and Hague, *An Introduction to the Courts and Judicial Process*, 40.
16. Abraham, *The Judicial Process*, 139–40.
17. Lewis, Bundy, and Hague, *An Introduction to the Courts and Judicial Process*, 40.
18. Abraham, *The Judicial Process*, 141–42.
19. Ibid., 142–43.
20. Edward C. Smith (Introduction), William R. Barnes (Notes and Charts), and Samuel Smith (Self-Scoring Examination), eds., *The Constitution of the United States* (New York: Barnes and Noble, 1936), 46. Complete text of the Constitution with index guide, Declaration of Independence, Articles of Confederation, and Virginia Bills of Rights.
21. Lewis, Bundy, and Hague, *An Introduction to the Courts and Judicial Process*, 56–58.
22. Abraham, *The Judicial Process*, 158–60.
23. Ibid., 162–65.
24. Ibid., 159–72.
25. Alexis de Tocqueville, *Democracy in America*, Vol. I (New Rochelle: Arlington House), 85–88. First published in Paris, France, in the middle of the 19th century.
26. Lewis, Bundy, and Hague, *An Introduction to the Courts and Judicial Process*, 58.
27. Abraham, *The Judicial Process*, 24.
28. Ibid., 25–30.
29. Ibid.
30. Ibid., 32.
31. Ibid., 48–50.
32. Ibid., 88–89.
33. James Willard Hurst, *The Growth of American Law—The Law Makers* (Boston: Little, Brown & Co., 1950), 18–19.
34. Thomas J. Gardner, *Criminal Evidence—Principles, Cases and Readings* (St. Paul: West Publishing Co., 1978), 2–3.

35. *Encyclopedia International*, Vol. X (20 Vols.; Lexicon Publications, Inc., 1979), 409–10.

36. David Humes, *The History of England: From the Invasion of Julius Caesar to the Abdication of James the Second, 1688* (Philadelphia: J.B. Lippincott & Co., 1754/1761), 70–71.

37. Ibid., 72–73.

38. Ibid., 165.

39. Ibid.

40. Dorothy Whitelock, ed., (David C. Douglas, General Editor), "King Athelstan's Laws Issued at Grately, Hampshire, 924–939 A.D.," *English Historical Documents*, Vol. I (15 Vols.; London, Eyre & Spottiswoode, 1968), 382.

41. Ibid., 385.

42. George W. Greenaway, ed., (David C. Douglas, General Editor), "The Laws of William the Conqueror," *English Historical Documents*, Vol. II (15 Vols.; London, Eyre & Spottiswoode, 1968), 399. This document appears in its earliest form in the "Textus Roffensis," ed., T. Horne (1720), a manuscript of the earlier half of the 12th century. It is probably a compilation of legal enactments made at various times by the Conqueror, apart from his confirmations of earlier laws and customs.

43. Greenaway, "Judicial Reforms of Henry II," 59.

44. Ibid., "The Assize of Clarendon," 407. The term "assize" has several meanings: a session of a legislative body or court, a decree or edict rendered at such a session, a judicial inquest, the writ by which it was instituted, the verdict of the jurors, or, one of the periodic court sessions which were held in each of the counties of England and Wales for the trial of civil and criminal cases.

45. Ibid., 407–8.

46. Ibid., 411.

47. Ibid., "Granville," *English Historical Documents* (15 Vols.; London, Eyre & Spottiswoode, 1968), 462. The legal treatise

known as "Granville," was actually entitled, "Concerning the Laws and Customs of the Kingdom of England: Methods of Trial in Operation during the Reign of Henry II." The treatise itself has been traditionally assigned to Rannulf de Glanville, Justiciar of England from 1180 A.D. to 1189 A.D., although others assign authorship to his nephew, Hubert Walter.

48. Ibid., "Concerning Ownership: Trial by Battle, and the Grand Assize," 464–66.
49. Ibid., 466–67.
50. Ibid., 468.
51. Ibid., 467.
52. Ibid., 469.
53. Ibid.; "Concerning Criminal Pleas Which Belong to the Crown," 476–77.
54. Ibid., 477.
55. Ibid., "Accounts of Henry II's Judicial Reforms," 478–79.
56. Ibid., 482.
57. Ibid., 58–59.

CHAPTER TWO

1. Merrill Jensen, ed. (David C. Douglas, General Editor), "American Colonial Documents to 1776," *English Historical Documents*, Vol. IX (15 Vols; New York: Oxford University Press, 1955), 167–69.
2. William Walker Hening, ed., *Virginia: The Statutes at Large; Being A Collection of all the Laws of Virginia, from the First Session of the Legislature in the year 1619*, Vol. I (10 Vols.; New York: R. & W. & G. Bartow, 1820–1823), iv. Published Pursuant to an Act of the General Assembly of Virginia, Passed on the Fifth Day of February One Thousand Eight Hundred and Eight. Thomas Jefferson, late President of the United States, has contributed more than any other individual to the preservation of our ancient laws. He very

early employed himself in collecting them for public use; and to his assistance the editor is chiefly indebted for the material which compose the present work. (Found in the Microbook Library of American Civilization—Subject Volume-LAC 20561-70).

3. Ibid., "Letters Patent From the King," 57.

4. Ibid., "Ancient Charters, Relating to the First Settlement of Virginia," 60, 64.

5. Ibid., 67–68.

6. Ibid., 68–69. The King had listed the offenses of "tumults, rebellion, conspiracies, mutiny and seditions, murder, manslaughter, incest, rape, and adulteries," previously in the Charter.

7. Ibid., 69–70.

8. Ibid., "Second Charter to the Treasurer and Company, for Virginia, Erecting Them Into a Corporation and Body Politic, and for the Further Enlargement and Explanation of the Privileges of the said Company and First Colony of Virginia, dated May 23, 1609," 80.

9. Ibid., Vol. V, 388–89. The 25th of March was the beginning of the year according to the Jewish computation; and the same rule was observed in England until by Stat. 24, Geo. 2, Chap. 23, Sect. 1 (1751), it was declared that after the last day of December 1751, the 25th of March should no longer be accounted by beginning of the year, but that the year 1752 should begin on the first day of January, and so, in each succeeding year, the first day of January should be deemed the first day of the year. This statute was rendered necessary by the adoption in England of the reformed calendar of Pope Gregory XIII, made in the year 1572; from which period commenced the Gregorian calendar, or New Style. Accordingly, in most of the dates prior to 1752, we see the old year continued until the 25th of March, with the new year annexed to it from the 1st of January to that date.

10. Ibid., "Third Charter of King James I to the Treasurer and Company, for Virginia, Dated March 12, 1611–2," Vol. I, 98.

11. Ibid., "First Session of the Virginia Legislature, 1619; Second Session of the Virginia Legislature, 1620; Third Session of the Virginia Legislature, 1621," 119.

12. Ibid., "An Ordinance and Constitution of the Treasurer Council, and Company in England, for a Council of State and General Assembly," 110–12.

13. Ibid., "Laws and Orders Concluded on by the General Assembly, March the 5th, 1623–4," 121. From a M.S. furnished the editor by Thomas Jefferson, President of the United States. This M.S. is endorsed, (evidently in the same handwriting with the acts themselves) thus—"The First Laws Made by the Assembly in Virginia, Anno MDC XXIII." Immediately underneath, in the handwriting of Mr. Jefferson, is this endorsement: "This was found among the manuscript papers of Sir John Randolph, and by the Honorable Peyton Randolph, Esq., his son, was given to Thomas Jefferson."

14. Ibid., "The Minutes of the Judicial Proceedings of the Governor and Council of Virginia," 145. (Found in the Ancient Records Relating to Virginia, Vol. 3, 125.)

15. Ibid., "Grand Assembly Holden Att James City, February 21, 1631–2," 168–69. From a M.S. belonging to Thomas Jefferson, President of the United States, purchased by him with the library of Peyton Randolph, from his executors. (Now in the Library of Congress.)

16. Ibid., "Grand Assembly Holden Att James City, March 16, 1642–3," 273. From a M.S. received from Edmund Randolph, Esq., which was once the property of Sir John Randolph, who transmitted it to his son, Peyton Randolph, Esq., after whose death, it was purchased, with his library, by Thomas Jefferson, Esq., from whom it was borrowed by Edmund Randolph, Esq.

17. Ibid., 273–74.
18. Ibid., 275.
19. Ibid., "Grand Assembly Holden Att James City, November 20, 1645," 303–04. (The records of this session were preserved in the same fashion as noted for the session in 1642–43.)
20. Ibid., 304.
21. Ibid., "Grand Assembly Holden Att James City, April 26, 1652," 369–72. (The records of this session were preserved in the same fashion as noted for the session in 1642–43.)
22. Ibid., "Grand Assembly Holden Att James City, March 10, 1655–6," 397–99.
23. Ibid., 402.
24. Ibid., "Grand Assembly Holden Att James City, March 13, 1657–8," 435.
25. Ibid., 466.
26. Ibid., "Grand Assembly Holden Att James City, March 7, 1658–9," 521–23.
27. Ibid., "Grand Assembly Holden Att James City, March 3, 1660–1," Vol. II, 21, 23. From a manuscript belonging to Thomas Jefferson, late President of the United States, and in his own handwriting; having been transcribed by him from the original, in the office of the Grand Assembly. (Now in the Library of Congress.)
28. William Brigham, ed., *New Plymouth Colony—Laws—Statutes & Compact* (Boston: Dutton & Wenworth, 1836), 19. The Compact with the Charter and laws of the colony of New Plymouth: together with the Charter of the Council at Plymouth, and an appendix containing the Articles of Confederation of the United Colonies of New England, and other valuable documents. (Found in the Microbook Library of American Civilization—Subject Volume—LAC 16280.)
29. Ibid, "The Charter of the Colony of New Plymouth," 21.
30. Ibid, "Laws of the Colony of New Plymouth, 1623," 28.

31. William T. Davis, ed., *Bradford's History of Plymouth Plantation, 1606–1646* (New York: Barnes & Noble, Inc., copyright 1908 by Charles Scribner & Sons. All Rights Assigned to Barnes & Nobles, Inc., 1946), 270–71.

32. Brigham, "Laws of the Colony of New Plymouth, 1633–36," *New Plymouth Colony*, 35–37.

33. Ibid., 38–42.

34. Ibid., 88.

35. James Kendall Hosmer, ed., *Winthrop's Journal, "History of New England,"* Vol. 1 (2 Vols.; New York: Barnes & Nobles, Inc., 1908), 55–62.

36. Ibid., 63, 122.

37. William H. Whitmore, ed., *The Colonial Laws of Massachusetts* (Boston: Published by order of the City Council of Boston under the supervision of Wm. H. Whitmore, Record Commissioner, 1887), 22. Citing the General Laws and Liberties of the Massachusetts Colony (Cambridge: Printed by Samuel Green for John Usher of Boston, 1672), and the Supplement Through 1686. (Found in the Microbook Library of American Civilization—Subject Volume—LAC 14744.)

38. Hosmer, *Winthrop's Journal, "History of New England,"* 122, 125.

39. Whitmore, *The Colonial Laws of Massachusetts*, 86–87.

40. Ibid.

41. Ibid.

42. Ibid., 38.

43. Hosmer, *Winthrop's Journal, "History of New England,"* 312–15.

44. Ibid., 237, 239.

45. Ibid., 323–24.

46. Whitmore, *The Colonial Laws of Massachusetts*, 36–39.

47. Ibid.

48. Ibid.

49. Ibid.
50. Ibid., 1.
51. Ibid., 3.
52. Ibid., 36–39.
53. Ibid., 152.
54. Ibid., 158–159.
55. Ibid., 152.
56. Ibid., 2–4.
57. Ibid., 158–59.
58. Ibid., 21.
59. Ibid.
60. Ibid., 5–8.

Chapter Three

1. Whitmore, *The Colonial Laws of Massachusetts*, 5–8, 21.
2. Hening, "Grand Assembly Holden Att James City, March 16, 1642–3," *Virginia: The Statutes at Large*, 273–75.
3. Vernon Louis Parrington, *The Colonial Mind, 1620–1800* (New York: Harcourt, Brace & World, Inc., 1927), 5–7.
4. Morris Talpalar, *The Sociology of Colonial Virginia* (New York: Philosophical Library, Inc., 1960), 79, 80–81, 103–05.
5. Hening, "Grand Assembly Holden Att James City, March 23, 1661," *Virginia: The Statutes at Large*, 58–59. From a M.S. presented to the editor by the Court of Northumberland County.
6. Ibid., 57–60.
7. Ibid., 63–64.
8. Ibid., 65–66.
9. Ibid., 67–69.
10. Ibid., 70.
11. Ibid., 72.
12. Ibid., 73–74.
13. Hening, "Grand Assembly Holden at James Cittie, December 23, 1662," *Virginia: The Statutes at Large*, 167–68.

14. Hening, "At a Grand Assembly Begun at Green Spring the 20th Day of February, Anno Dni, 1676–7," *Virginia: The Statutes at Large*, 384.

15. Hening, "Grand Assembly, Begunn at Middle Plantation att the House of Capt. Otho Thorpe, the 10th Day of Ocotober, ANNO DOMINI, 1677," *Virginia: The Statutes at Large*, 422.

16. Hening, "At A Grand Assembly Begunn at James Citty the 25th of April, ANNO DOMINI 1679," *Virginia: The Statutes at Large*, 441–42.

17. Hening, "Att A Grand Assembly Begun at James Citty, April 16, 1684," *Virginia: The Statutes at Large*, Vol. III (Philadelphia: Printed for the editor by Thomas DeSilver), 10.

18. Ibid., "An Act for the More Speedy Prosecution of Slaves Committing Capital Crimes," "Grand Assembly Holden at James Citty, April 16, 1692," 102.

19. Ibid., "Summon for Deposition," "Att A General Court Begun att James Citty, September 24, 1696," 145.

20. Ibid., "Qualifications of Jurors," "At A General Assembly Begun at James Citty, the 27th Day of April, 1699," 176.

21. Ibid., "A New Court—A Court of Claims," "General Assembly Begun at James Citty, October 1705," 261–62.

22. Ibid., "An Act for the Speedy & Easy Prosecution of Slaves Committing Capital Crimes," 269–70.

23. Ibid., "Witnesses in General Court," 297.

24. Ibid., "Witnesses to be Free From Arrest," 299.

25. Ibid., "An Act Concerning Juries," 367.

26. Although the Virginia Statutes revealed no evidence that the General Assembly was formally deprived of its role as the judicial court of last resort; the powers conferred by the 1662 assembly to the county courts, and to the General Court, did in fact, nullify any future role as an active judicial participant. The establishment at the county level of the courts for proof

of public claims in 1705, retrieved a quasi-judicial role for the assembly; although in practice, even this small morsel was weakened by the "implied" infrequency of the assembly to overrule the court's decisions.

27. Extensive and exhaustive research has convincingly determined the following fact: that an appellate tribunal of last resort—allegedly entitled the "Court of Oyer and Terminer"—was not established as the supreme court of Virginia in 1710, as claimed by the textbook, entitled, "An Introduction to the Courts and Judicial Process," page 10. Furthermore, there is no record of such a court being established in Virginia at any time prior to 1778. The only references to the terminology of "Oyer and Terminer" prior to the date of 1778, and on or about the year of 1710, is located in the Virginia Statutes as below noted. Footnote #19 of this chapter, stated that, "—governor is impowered to issue out commission of Oyer and Terminer directing such persons of said counties as he shall think fit..." and, "An Act to Explain Part of An Act of Assembly, Intituled An Act for Establishing the General Court, and for Regulating & Settling the Proceeding Therein," At A General Assembly Begun & Holden at the Capital, in the City of Williamsburg, October 1710, Vol. IV, page 492: "That nothing in the said Act contained, shall be construed, deemed, or taken to derogate from, less, or abridge the Royal powers, prerogative, and authority of her Majesty, her heirs and successors of granting commission or commissions of oyer and terminer, or of constituting and erecting such other court or courts of record, as her majesty...for the time being, shall direct, order or appoint."

28. Hening, "Courts of Hustings," "General Assembly Begun October 1705," *Virginia: The Statutes at Large*, Vol. III, 407–10.

29. Hening, "Courts of Records," *Virginia: The Statutes at Large*, Vol. III, 302.

30. Hening, "State Houses," *Virginia: The Statutes at Large*, Vol. III, 412.

31. Hening, "Jurisdiction of County Courts in Probate of Mills and Administrations," "General Assembly Begun at Williamsburg, November 7, 1711," *Virginia: The Statutes at Large*, Vol. IV, 12. (From Edition 1733, 270.)

32. Hening, "When General Courts May Grant Probate," *Virginia: The Statutes at Large*, Vol. IV, 28.

33. Hening, "An Act for Setting the Fees of the Court Secretarys, County Court Clerks, Sheriffs, Corners, and Constables; and for Ascertaining the Fees of Attorneys," "General Assembly Begun at Williamsburg, April 23, 1718," *Virginia: The Statutes at Large*, Vol. IV, 59.

34. Hening, "Summons for a Defendant to Appear," "At A General Assembly, Begun and Held At Williamsburg, the 1st Day of February, 1727," *Virginia: The Statutes at Large*, Vol. IV, 182–84.

35. Hening, "Defendant in Custody May Plead to Issue," *Virginia: The Statutes at Large*, Vol. IV, 185.

36. Ibid.

37. Hening, "Procedure to Outlaw a Defendant of Civil Suit," *Virginia: The Statutes at Large*, Vol. IV, 186.

38. Hening, "For the Better Execution of the Laws Now in Force," "At A General Assembly Begun and Held at Williamsburg, May 21, 1730," *Virginia: The Statutes at Large*, Vol. IV, 243.

39. Hening, "An Act for Enforcing the Act, Instituted, An Act for the Effective Suppression of Vice; and Restraint and Punishment of Blasphemous, Wicked and Dissolute Persons; And for Preventing Incestuous Marriages and Copulations," *Virginia: The Statutes at Large*, Vol. IV, 244–45.

40. Hening, "Book of A Dead Person," "At A General Assembly Begun and Held at Williamsburg, May 1732," *Virginia: The Statutes at Large*, Vol. IV, 328.

41. Hening, "Act for Regulating Admisssion to the Practice of Law," *Virginia: The Statutes at Large*, Vol. IV, 360–61.

42. Hening, "Absent Defendants—How Preceeded Against in Chancery," "At A General Assembly Begun and Held at Williamsburg, September 4, 1744," *Virginia: The Statutes at Large*, Vol. IV, 220–21.

43. Hening, "Defendants Refusing to Make An Appearance," *Virginia: The Statutes at Large*, Vol. IV, 222.

44. Hening, "Presentment of the Grand Juries," *Virginia: The Statutes at Large*, Vol. IV, 226.

45. Hening, "Appeal From the Justice of the Peace," *Virginia: The Statutes at Large*, Vol. IV, 230.

46. Hening, "Want of Form (conviction) No Bar," *Virginia: The Statutes at Large*, Vol. IV, 231.

47. Hening, "Christian Indians, Free Negroes and Mulatoes Can Be Witnesses," *Virginia: The Statutes at Large*, Vol. IV, 245.

48. Hening, "Powers of the General Court," "At A General Assembly, Begun and Held at the College in the City of Williamsburg, February 27, 1753," *Virginia: The Statutes at Large*, Vol. V, 327.

49. Ibid., 330.

50. Hening, "Appeals to the General Court," "At A General Assembly Begun and Held at Williamsburg, November 1, 1753," *Virginia: The Statutes at Large*, Vol. V, 340–42.

51. Hening, "Method of Obtaining Writs of Certiorari," *Virginia: The Statutes at Large*, Vol. V, 340–42.

52. Hening, "Habeas Corpus," *Virginia: The Statutes at Large*, Vol. V, 342.

53. Hening, "Juries for the General Court," *Virginia: The Statutes at Large*, Vol. V, 349.

54. Hening, "Committee of Safety," "At a Convention of Delegates Held at the Town of Richmond, in the Colony of Virginia, on Friday, the First of December, in the Year of Our Lord one thousand seven hundred and seventy-five, and afterwards, by adjournment, in the City of Williamsburg," *Virginia: The Statutes at Large*, Vol. IX, 105–06.

55. Hening, "Court of the Admiralty," *Virginia: The Statutes at Large*, Vol. IX, 103–04.

CHAPTER FOUR

1. Hening, "Virginia Bills of Rights Adopted on 12 June, 1776," "At a General Convention of Delegates & Representatives From the Several Counties & Corporations of Virginia, at the Capital, in the City of Williamsburg, on Monday the 6th of May, 1776," *Virginia: The Statutes at Large*, Vol. IX, 48.

2. James M. Smith and Paul L. Murphy, eds., "George Mason, The Virginia Declaration of Rights, June 12, 1776," *Liberty and Justice, Forging the Federal Union: American Constitutional Development to 1869* (2 Vols.; New York: Alfred A. Knoff, Inc., 1965), 50.

3. Ibid., 51.

4. S.E. Morison, ed., "The Constitution of Virginia, 29 June 1776," *Sources and Documents illustrating the American Revolution, 1764–1788, and the formation of the Federal Constitution* (London: Oxford University Press, Amen House, 1923), 151–56.

5. Oyer and Terminer: A hearing or trial; in the United States, a designation occasionally used for a high criminal court; in Great Britain, a commission to a judge by which he is empowered to hear and rule on a criminal case at the assizes; the court in which such a hearing is held; Middle English, from Norman French "oyer es terminer," "to hear and determine." (Found in the American Heritage Dictionary.)

6. Hening, "At a General Assembly Held at the Capital, in Williamsburg, May 1776," *Virginia: The Statutes at Large*, Vol. IX, 172.

7. Hening, "Committee of Safety," "At a Convention of Delegates Held at the Town of Richmond, in the Colony of Virginia, on Friday, the First of December, the Year of Our Lord one thousand seven hundred and seventy-five, and afterwards, by adjournment, in the City of Williamsburg," *Virginia: The Statutes at Large*, Vol. IX, 105–06.

8. Ibid., 105-06, 172–73.

9. Ibid., 172–173.

10. Hening, "Resolutions Allowing Resumption of Lawsuits," "At a General Assembly Begun and Held At the Capital, in the City of Williamsburg, May 5, 1777," *Virginia: The Statutes at Large*, Vol. IX, 368.

11. Hening, "An Act for Establishing a High Court of Chancery," "At a General Assembly Begun and Held at the Capital, in the City of Williamsburg, October 1777," *Virginia: The Statutes at Large*, Vol. IX, 389. A court with jurisdiction in equity, as distinguished from one with jurisdiction in common law; applying justice in litigative circumstances not covered by law.

12. Hening, "An Act for Establishing a General Court," *Virginia: The Statutes at Large*, Vol. IX, 389–390.

13. Ibid., 401–02.

14. Ibid., 44, 401–02.

15. Hening, "Witnesses of the General Court," *Virginia: The Statutes at Large*, Vol. IX, 410.

16. Ibid., 411–12.

17. Ibid., 410.

18. Ibid., 411–12.

19. Ibid.

20. Hening, "Writ of Supersedeas," *Virginia: The Statutes at Large*, Vol. IX, 412–13.

21. Hening, "Writ of Certiorari," *Virginia: The Statutes at Large*, Vol. IX, 413.

22. Hening, "Writ of Habeas Corpus," *Virginia: The Statutes at Large*, Vol. IX, 414.

23. Hening, "Statutes of Limitations Applicable to the General Court," *Virginia: The Statutes at Large*, Vol. IX, 414.

24. Hening "Examining Court," *Virginia: The Statutes at Large*, Vol. IX, 414–15; and Adrienne Kock and William Peden, eds., *The Life and Selected Writings of Jefferson* (New York: The Modern Library, Random House, 1940), 248, citing Thomas Jefferson, Notes on the State of Virginia, written in the year 1781, modified in the winter of 1782, for the use of the Marquis de Barbe—Marbois, Secretary of the French Legation in Philadelphia, in answer to inquiries about Virginia—first published in Paris, France, in 1784, at Jefferson's own expense.

25. Hening, "Criminal Trial Jury in General Court," "At a General Assembly Begun and Held at the Capital, in the City of Williamsburg, October 1977," *Virginia: The Statutes at Large*, Vol. IX, 416.

26. Adriene Koch and William Peden, eds., *The Life and Selected writings of Jefferson* (New York: Random House, 1944), 248, citing "Notes on the State of Virginia."

27. Ibid.; and Hening, "Rights and Expenses of Defendants," "At a General Assembly Began and Held at the Capital, in the City of Williamsburg, October 1777," *Virginia: The Statutes at Large*, Vol. IX, 416–17.

28. Hening, "General Court Sessions," "At a General Assembly Begun and Held at the Capital in the City of Williamsburg, May 1778," *Virginia: The Statutes at Large*, Vol. IX, 461.

29. Hening, "Length of Incarceration without Trial," "At a General Assembly Begun and Held at the Capital in Williamsburg, October 1778," *Virginia: The Statutes at Large*, Vol. IX, 474.

30. Hening, "An Act for Establishing a Court of Appeals," *Virginia: The Statutes at Large*, Vol. IX, 522–23.
31. Hening, "Jurisdiction of the Court of Appeals," *Virginia: The Statutes at Large*, Vol. IX, 523.
32. Smith and Murphy, "The Articles of Confederation and Perpetual Union," *Liberty and Justice*, 54.
33. Ibid.
34. Ibid., 45–47.
35. Smith, Barnes, and Smith, *The Constitution of the United States*, 46.
36. Ibid.
37. Ibid., 15.
38. Smith and Murphy, "The Constitution of the United States," *Liberty and Justice*, 62.
39. Morison, "Selections From Debates in the Virginia Ratifying Convention, June 1788," *Sources and Documents*, 340–42.
40. Ibid., 342–43.
41. James Madison, Alexander Hamilton, and John Jay, "A View of the Constitution of the Judicial Department in Relation to the Tenture of Good Bahvior," *The Federalist Papers* (New Rochelle: Arlington House), 466–67. This Heirloom Edition of The Federalist Papers is taken from the first edition, the famous McLean Edition of 1788. This particular article was authored by Alexander Hamilton.
42. Smith and Murphy, "The Judiciary Act of 1789, September 24, 2789," *Liberty and Justice*, 87.
43. Ibid.
44. Ibid., 87–88.
45. Ibid.
46. Paul C. Bartholomew, ed., "Marbury v. Madison, 1 Cranch 137; 2 L. Ed. 60 (1803)," *Summaries of Leading Cases on the Constitution* (Totowa: Littlefield, Adams & Co., 1968), 166–67.

47. Ibid.

48. Ibid., 167–68.

CHAPTER FIVE

1. Peter S. DuPonceau, *A Dissertation on the Nature and Extent of the Jurisdiction of the Courts of the United States* (Philadelphia: Published by Abraham Small, 1824), vii. This was a valedictory address delivered to the students of the Law Academy of Philadelphia, at the close of the academic year, on the 22nd of April, 1824. Published the second time by the Arno Press, New York, 1972, as part of the *American Law: The Formative Years Series.*

2. Ibid., vii–viii.

3. Ibid., ix.

4. Ibid., x–xi

5. Ibid., xii–xiv.

6. John Milton Goodenow, *Historical Sketches of the Principles and Maxims of American Jurisprudence in Contrast with the Doctrines of the English Common Law or the Subject's Crimes and Punishments* (Steubenville: Printed by James Wilson, 1819), vi. Published the second time by the Arno Press, New York, 1972, as part of the *American Law: The Formative Years Series.*

7. Ibid., 14.

8. Ibid., 17–18.

9. Ibid., 18–19.

10. Ibid., 19–20.

11. Ibid.

12. Ibid., 32–33.

13. Ibid., 35–36.

14. Zephaniah Swift, *A Digest of the Law of Evidence in Civil and Criminal Cases and a Treatise of Bills of Exchanges and Promissory Notes* (Hartford: Published by Oliver D. Clark, 1810), iv. Published for the second time by the Arno Press,

New York, 1972, as part of the *American Law: The Formative Years Series*. Mr. Swift at the time of the aforementioned date, was a judge of the Supreme Court of the State of Connecticut.

15. Ibid.
16. Ibid., viii.
17. Ibid., x.
18. Tocqueville, *Democracy in America*, 83–85.
19. Ibid.
20. Ibid., 86.
21. Ibid., 87–88.
22. Ibid., 91–93.
23. The author's conclusions.
24. Parrington, *The Colonial Mind 1620–1800*, 5–8.
25. Ibid., 8–11.
26. Ibid., 16–17.
27. Talpalar, *The Sociology of Virginia*, 20–23.
28. The author's conclusions.
29. Parrington, *The Colonial Mind 1620–1800*, 17.
30. Ibid., 17–23.
31. Ibid., 22; and, Goodenow, *Historical Sketches*, 208.
32. Talpalar, *The Sociology of Virginia*, 65, 74–82, 104.
33. Goodnenow, *Historical Sketches*, 180–82.
34. Ibid., 256.
35. Ibid., 268.
36. Jensen, "American Colonial Documents to 1776," *English Historical Documents*, 167.
37. Ibid., 168–69.
38. Charles Francis Adams, ed., *The Works of John Adams* (Boston: Little, Brown & Co., 1850–56), 19–21. Second President of the United States, his notes, illustrations, etc., were drawn together by his grandson.
39. Talpalar, *The Sociology of Colonial Virginia*, 103–05.
40. The author's conclusions.

41. Harold P. Simonson, ed., *Significance of the Frontier In American History by Frederick Jackson Turner* (New York: Frederick Ungar Publishing Co., 1963), 9–11.
42. Ibid., 12.
43. Ibid., 51.
44. The author's conclusions.

BIBLIOGRAPHY

Abraham, Henry J. *The Judicial Process: An Introductory Analysis of the Courts of the United States, England, and France*. New York: Oxford University Press, 1975.

Adams, Charles Francis, ed. *The Works of John Adams*. Boston: Little, Brown & Co., 1850–1856. Found in the Microbook Library of American Civilization—Subject Volume—LAC 20283.

Bartholomew, Paul C., ed. *Summaries of Leading Cases of the Constitution*. Totowa: Littlefield, Adams & Co., 1968.

Brigham, William, ed. *New Plymouth Colony—Laws—Statutes—Compact*. Boston: Dutton & Wenworth, 1836. Found in the Microbook Library of American Civilization—Subject Volume—LAC 16280.

Davis, Willim T., ed. *Bradford's History of Plymouth Plantation 1606–1646*. New York: Barnes & Nobles, Inc., 1946. Originally published 1908 by Charles Scribner & Sons.

de Tocqueville, Alexis. *Democracy in America*. New Rochelle: Arlington House, Translated by Henry Reeve.

DuPonceau, Peter S. *A Dissertation on the Nature and Extent of the Jurisdiction of the Courts of the United States*. New York: Arno Press, 1972. Originally published 1824 in Philadelphia by Abraham Small.

Encyclopedia International. Vol. 10. Lexicon Publications, Inc., 1979.

Gardner, Thomas J. *Criminal Evidence—Principles, Cases and Readings*. St. Paul: West Publishing Co., 1978.

Goodenow, John Milton. *Historical Sketches of the Principles and Maxims of American Jurisprudence in Contrast With the Doctrine of the English Common Law or the Subject's Crimes and Punishments*. New York: Arno Press, 1972. Originally published 1819 in Steubenville by James Wilson.

Greenaway, George W., ed. *English Historical Documents, Vol. II, 1042–1189*. London: Eyre & Spottiswoode, 1968.

Hening, William Walker, ed. *Virginia: The Statutes at Large; Being a Collection of all the Laws of Virginia, from the First Session of the Legislature in the Year 1619*. New York: R. & W. & G. Bartow, 1820–1823. Found in the Microbook Library of American Civilization—Subject Volume—LAC 20561–70.

Hosmer, James Kendall, ed. *Winthrop's Journal—History of New England*. 2 Vols. New York: Barnes & Nobles, Inc., 1908.

Hume, David. *The History of England From the Invasion of Julius Casar to the Abdication of James the Second, 1688*. Philadelphia: J.B. Lippincott & Co., 1754–1761.

Hurst, James Willard. *The Growth of American Law—The Law Makers*. Boston: Little, Brown & Co., 1950.

Jensen, Merrill, ed. *English Historical Documents, Vol. IX, American Colonial Documents to 1776*. New York: Oxford University Press, 1955.

Koch, Adriene, and William Peden, eds. *The Life and Selected Writings of Jefferson*. New York: Random House, 1944.

Lewis, Merlin; Warren Bundy; and, James L. Hague. *An Introduction to the Courts and Judicial Process*. Englewood Cliffs: Prentice-Hall Inc., 1978.

Madison, James; Alexander Hamilton; and, John Jay. *The Federalist Papers*. New Rochelle: Arlington House. First published as the famous McLean Edition in 1788.

Morison, S.E., ed. *Sources and Documents, Illustrating the American Revolution 1764–1788 and the Formation of the Federal Constitution.* London: Oxford University Press, 1923.

Parrington, Vernon Louis. *The Colonial Mind.* New York: Harcourt, Brace & World, Inc., 1927.

Simonson, Harold P., ed. *The Significance of the Fronter in American History,* by Frederick Jackson Turner. New York: Frederick Ungar Publishing Co., Inc., 1963.

Smith, James M., and Paul L. Murphy, eds. *Liberty and Justice, Forging the Federal Union: American Constitutional Development to 1869.* 2 Vols. New York: Alfred A. Knoff, Inc., 1958.

Swift, Zephaniah. *A Digest of the Laws of Evidence in Civil and Criminal Cases and a Treatise on Bills of Exchanges and Promissory Notes.* New York: Arno Press, 1972. Originally published 1810 in Hartford by Peter B. Gleason.

Talpalar, Morris. *The Sociology of Virginia.* New York: Philosophical Library Inc., 1960.

The Constitution of the United States. Introduction by Edward C. Smith, Notes and Charts by William R. Barnes, and Self-Scoring Examination by Samuel Smith. New York: Barnes & Noble, Inc., 1936.

Whitlock, Dorothy, ed. *English Historical Documents, Vol. I, 500–1042.* London: Eyre & Spottiswoode, 1968.

Whitmore, William H., ed. *The Colonial Laws of Massachusetts.* Boston: Printed by Samuel Green, 1672. Found in the Microbook Library of American Civilization—Subject Volume—LAC 14744.

CPSIA information can be obtained
at www.ICGtesting.com
Printed in the USA
FSHW020417020222
88072FS

9 781737 886419